# SELF-PUBLISHING IN GERMAN

### How to translate, publish and market your books

## SKYE B. MACKINNON

Peryton Press

# CONTENTS

## PREPARING TO PUBLISH

## PUBLISHING CHOICES

### Part 1
### RETAILERS

### Part 2
### DISTRIBUTORS

**Part 3**
**PRINT BOOKS**

**Part 4**
**AUDIOBOOKS**

# MARKETING

# FOREWORD

Dear reader,

Take a deep breath and let go of everything you know about the book market. You're about to enter a new, exciting world full of surprises that will make you rethink everything you've learned during your self-publishing journey. Well, not everything, but a lot.

Entering a new market in a new language isn't easy. You don't simply hire a translator and publish whatever they give you, then forget about it. Sorry if that bursts your bubble.

This is going to be hard work. You're going to have to invest time, money and elbow grease into this process.

Not that this is news for you, a self-published author juggling writing with marketing and admin tasks. You'll be used to hiring professionals, outsourcing some aspects of your publishing life while doing others yourself. You'll be used to constantly learning new techniques that make your writing and your publishing better. You'll be used to researching solutions to problems you come across.

You already have the skills you need - you just need to apply them in a slightly new way to succeed with your German adventure.

This book will guide you through the process, giving you as much information as possible about the entire process, starting with hiring a translator all the way to marketing your book to German-speaking readers. Of course, everyone's journey is unique. What works for some might not work for you, while you might find successes that others can't replicate.

I don't pretend to know everything. My knowledge has built through trial and error, lots of research, many hours spent trawling through forums and Facebook groups. I've made copious mistakes, but I've learnt from them and hope you can learn from them in turn.

I hope this book will help you in bringing your book to a new market - good luck und viel Glück!

*Skye B. MacKinnon*

perytonpress.com

FREE printable
self-publishing
dictionary

# BEFORE WE BEGIN

As you'll be aware, the publishing world changes all the time. What works this year might be very different next year already. I have tried to keep this guide as timeless as possible and I will update it from time to time.

## SURVEY: WHAT OTHER AUTHORS DID

As part of the research for this book, I did a little mini-survey with other authors who've had their books translated into German. Twenty people took part, so while the results aren't necessarily representative, they are certainly interesting.

Amazingly, a third of the authors I polled have published 10 or more German translations already - very impressive.

Throughout this book, I will refer to the results of this survey to give you an idea of what other (successful) authors did.

## SOME HOUSEKEEPING NOTICES:

- While this book is about publishing and marketing German-language book, it doesn't focus on only Germany as a country. However, to keep things short, I will occasionally call all German-language marketplaces the German market. To avoid confusion, I will always highlight if something is specific to Germany alone.
- For some services, I mention prices. These are of course subject to change. You'll often have to add VAT (19% standard, reduced to 7% for some products and services including books).
- This book will touch on several legal issues like copyright, contracts and imprints. I'm not a lawyer and I don't claim to be one. While I have done my best to make sure that everything is correct, I can't guarantee it and always recommend consulting a (German) lawyer if you have questions.
- Many of the websites I link to are in German - I always clearly label them as such. I recommend using Google Chrome's inbuilt translation feature to browse those sites, although of course other browsers and software have similar options.
- This book is written in British English.
- All links to service providers and resources are working at time of publication, but of course there's no guarantee they will still be operating in a year's time. If you find a broken link, please email me at skye@perytonpress.com.

*Please note: Some of the links to products and services in this book are referral links, which means I might receive a small percentage of a potential sale at no extra cost to you. Most of these links are clearly labelled as referral links.*

# INTRODUCTION

# 1

## WHY GERMAN?

I n 1440, a German goldsmith called Johannes Gutenberg
started a revolution.

Until this moment in history, books had been restricted to
the church, the nobility and the wealthy. They were copied
by hand or by woodblock printing, making them
inaccessible and unaffordable for the masses. Gutenberg's
invention, a mechanical movable-type printing press,
changed that, allowing the mass production of books. In a
day, the Gutenberg press could print several thousand
pages, compared to forty by hand-printing and just a
handful when copied by hand.

The invention would alter society forever. Suddenly,
information transcended classes and borders, aiding the
spread of new ideas and threatening the power of religious
and political authorities.

Books gave people power. With rising literacy, education
was no longer restricted to the elite. The printing press fed

the growing Renaissance and later instigated the scientific revolution.

From Germany, the printing press spread across Europe. Authorship became important. Storytelling and oral reading for families and groups turned into private reading, just the book and its reader. The first bestsellers emerged. Philosopher Erasmus sold over 750,000 copies of his works during his lifetime.

Several centuries later and Germany is still the home of avid readers. Germans spend the second-most in Europe on books, newspapers and stationary, 1.6% of household expenditure (second only to Slovakia). In the US, it's only 0.146%.

In 2019, the German book market was worth 7.63 billion Euro (4.6 billion of that was fiction) - more than twice as much as in the UK and more than three times as much as in Spain or Italy (should you be considering those languages for translations).

The average German spends 5.7 hours a week reading (less than Australia, same as the US, more than the UK) and reads 8-10 books a year.

Wouldn't you want one of those books to be yours?

Good news for you: 14% of newly released books in German are translations, almost two thirds of them from English. Readers are used to translated books - however, this also means they expect them to be just as good as books written in Germany. They will be hard on you if your translations is bad, and I mean, *really* hard. We'll talk more about how to make sure your translator is up to scratch later.

## 2

## MY EXPERIENCE

Time to tell you a little bit about my own translation experience. I write both romance (as Skye MacKinnon) and books for children (as Isla Wynter), which gave me the opportunity to experiment with translations for several genres.

At this point I should probably mention that I'm bilingual and grew up in Germany. I experienced the German book market (and the library!) as a book-hungry child and teenager, so I've seen it from the consumer side. After leaving Germany, I lived in several different countries before settling in Scotland over a decade ago. All my books are written in English and I only knew the English-speaking publishing world before embarking on the quest to have some of my books translated.

Speaking German has certainly helped me immensely - but I didn't do my translations myself. My grammar isn't what it used to be (as my grandma likes to tell me) and even if it was up to scratch, I simply wouldn't have had the time. Translating a book can take as long as writing it or even longer. But if you now think that you won't have a chance if you don't speak German, don't worry. There are ways around this and we'll talk about all that in detail.

Back to that quest. I started my translation journey in late 2018 and after a lot of research and planning published my first translation in March 2019. It was one of my picture books, which made it fairly fast and cheap – perfect for learning the ropes, exploring different retailers and discovering how marketing differed from what I was used to. When I saw how well the book was selling, I had more of my children's books translated, before finally moving on to my adult books in 2020. I decided to start with my most popular series, an urban fantasy with a slow burn romance. It has a lot of evergreen tropes and already sold occasional copies in German-language markets. While it's my longest series with seven books in total, the first big story arch ends after book four, so in case the translations didn't sell well, I could have stopped at that point without leaving readers feeling that they didn't get a complete series.

I waited until my translator was done with the first two books so I could publish them without too much of a wait in between. I left a three-week gap between those two, then published a new translation every two months until the series was completed a year later.

To my surprise, I broke even within the first few weeks of publishing the first book. Translations suddenly made up almost two thirds of my total income. I ended up on several retailers' bestseller lists, increasing visibility and leading even more readers to try my books. I'd been in touch with the marketing team at tolino and they added my book to a whole bunch of promotions, including showcasing it as the 'indie book of the week' at one retailer.

Anyway, it was a great start. Looking back now, there are many things I would have done differently - which is why I'm writing this book. I wish I'd had a guide when I began looking into translations, so I'm partly writing this for past-me, naive and lost in the jungle of information, and everyone else who feels the same.

**3**

# WHY YOU SHOULDN'T GET YOUR BOOK TRANSLATED

Wait, what? Isn't this book all about turning your book into a German bestseller?

Yes - but with some caveats.

You need to be aware of what you commit to before you start this long, exciting journey. Are you ready at this point in time? Or would it be better to wait a bit?

1. **Translations are expensive.**

Very expensive. Do you have the money to not just translate one book, but an entire series? It could take months or even years to break even. Readers hate nothing more than incomplete series. By now, German readers have become wary of indie authors who may not get all the books in a series translated.

(Pro tip: set up pre-orders for all the books in your series to readers can see that they will definitely be published.)

. . .

## 2. **Translations take a lot of time and effort.**

While you aren't the one doing the actual translation, that doesn't mean you can twiddle your thumbs and watch the world go by. Finding translators, editors, proofreaders, beta readers, reviewers, bloggers, authors to cross-promote with,... all takes time. You will have to do research, vet a translator to make sure they can do what they promise, and even once you finally have your translation, the work doesn't end there.

## 3. **Marketing in another language is hard**

Consider this scenario: You have a new release. You know all the things you usually do: post on social media, send a newsletter, maybe do some ads. You might even do a blog tour or get influencers involved. Make a mental list of all your release day tasks. Then think of how many of these you could do in German. If you speak the language, good for you! You've just moved to the top of the class. But if you don't, you'll need help: people to translate your newsletter and your social media posts and all the other things you need to communicate with your readers. That takes time and money.

## 4. **You're back to basics**

No matter how popular and successful you are with your English books, with your translations, you start at the very beginning once again. You don't have a loyal following. You don't have a large newsletter list. Readers don't know you. Basically, you've just turned into a newbie author who will struggle to get their books seen by readers. Yes, you may have more knowledge and experience than a complete newbie, but that only helps to a certain extent. Did I mention this will take a lot of time?

Now that I've destroyed all your hopes and enthusiasm, let me tell you: it can be a wonderful, enriching (in more ways than one) experience. You'll explore a new market, find new readers, learn about a different culture, and hopefully increase your income.

Is it a journey for everyone? No.

Is it a journey for you? Only you can decide that.

# 4

# 10 FACTS YOU DIDN'T KNOW ABOUT GERMAN

While you don't need to speak German to have your books translated into German, it does help to have a little understanding of how the language works. Luckily, both English and German are Germanic languages and have a lot in common (more than you'd think!). In fact, the two languages share more than half of their vocabulary.

Don't believe me? Take a look at these translations:

Mouse - Maus
House - Haus
Garden - Garten
Lamp - Lampe
Man - Mann
Telephone - Telefon
Father - Vater

Here are some other things you may not know about German and that will come in handy during your translation journey. You can also find a mini-dictionary at the end of this book.

1. German is the 11th most widely spoken language in the world with 100 million native speakers and the most widely spoken mother language in the European Union. It's the official language of Germany (bet you never guessed that!), Austria, Switzerland and Liechtenstein, but is also a co-official language in Belgium, Luxembourg, South Tyrol in Italy, and Namibia. In addition to that, there are German-speaking communities in Eastern Europe and South America.

2. German differentiates between a formal and an informal 'you'. This is especially important in business settings.

• Sie (formal): used to address adults who you've only just met or who haven't invited you to switch to the informal 'du'. Sometimes, you'll have to wait a long time for that invitation - my German grandma still uses Sie with people she's known for decades. It's custom for the older or more senior person to suggest switching to the informal you.

• Du (informal): used between friends, family members and occasionally colleagues. Nowadays, younger people (and authors) will often address each other with 'du' even if they don't know each other. Still, it's always safest to start with 'Sie'.

3. All nouns are capitalised with no exceptions.

. . .

4. German words have three genders: masculine, feminine and neuter. Confusingly, a word's gender doesn't always correspond to the gender of the meaning of the word. For example, das Mädchen (the girl) uses the neuter even though a girl is clearly female.

If you know other Romance languages that use genders like French or Spanish and hope that they all use the same ones, you're out of luck. A word with a female gender in German might have a masculine gender in French.

5. Dates are written as DAY.MONTH.YEAR, e.g. 14.02.2021. When combining a day with a written-out month, use a full stop and a space after the day, e.g. 14. Februar.

6. Prices are written with the currency symbol after the price and instead of a fullstop, a comma is used before decimals, e.g. 2,99€. Germany and Austria both use the Euro (€ or EUR) as their currency while Switzerland and Liechtenstein use the Swiss franc (CHF).

7. German uses four letters you may not be familiar with: ä, ö, ü and ß. The first three are umlaut letters which cause the back vowels a, o and u to be shifted forward in the mouth to turn into /ɛ/, /ø/ and /y/.

The ß is called 'Eszett' and is a consonant presenting a double-s. You'll never find it at the beginning of a sentence. While in some cases it can be exchanged with 'ss', in other cases that would change the meaning of the word.

E.g. Masse = mass or crowd, Maße = measurements.

But how to type these characters? If you're on a Mac, you simply have to hold down a, o, u or s and a menu will appear that lets you choose the umlaut.

It's a little more difficult on Windows. Hold down the 'alt' key and type one of these codes:

• ä : Alt + 0228

• ö : Alt + 0246

• ü : Alt + 0252

• ß : Alt + 0223

• Ä : Alt + 0196

• Ö : Alt + 0214

• Ü : Alt + 0220

On some phones, you can long-press the corresponding letters to get a pop-up.

8. Like all languages, German is constantly evolving. In the past few decades - although it's been going on for longer, especially during the Allied occupation of West Germany after World War II - more and more English words have entered the average German's vocabulary, leading to something called Denglisch (the love child of Deutsch and English). You'll find words like Jeep, Quiz, Cornflakes, Groupie, Boss, and many others that mean exactly what you think.

But be aware of false friends! Some words in German that are taken from English actually mean something different.

My favourite example is Handy, the German word for mobile phone (cell phone for my American friends). Yes, it's handy to have a Handy, but Germans are often confused when they discover that the English-speaking world doesn't use the word to mean mobile phone.

9. You'll probably have come across very, very long German words that seem to look like gibberish. These massive words are compound words which consist of at least two words fused together. In English, you'd usually put a space or hyphen between these words, but in German, you turn them into one big monstrosity.

There are various contenders for the longest word. Here's one with a grandiose 79 letters: Donaudampfschiffahrtse-lektrizitätenhauptbetriebswerkbauunter-beamtengesellschaft meaning "association of subordinate officials of the head office management of the Danube steamboat electrical services", a variation on the "Donaudampfschifffahrtsgesellschaftskapitän" made popular by Mark Twain. Obviously, this word isn't one used in everyday language, but it's always fun to make up your own giant words (if you speak German, that is).

10. There are no silent letters. In English, many words have letters that aren't actually pronounced (leading to headaches for anyone learning English). In some words, the first letter isn't pronounced (e.g. psychology, knee) while in others, the last letter is ignored (e.g. comb, hate). Let's not get started on the pronunciation of some place names like Leicester (Lester) or Gloucester (Gloster).

In German, every letter is pronounced as it should be. While you will find some very long compound words in German, you can be sure that at least they aren't stuffed with silent letters.

If you want to get a feel for the language, I suggest you take a few lessons. There are various apps you can use or try some of the courses mentioned below.

---

## Resources

- Free BBC online course: https://www.bbc.co.uk/languages/german/
- Free online course by Deutsche Welle: https://learngerman.dw.com/en/overview
- Duolingo App: https://invite.duolingo.com/BDHTZTB5CWWKTVBZXHS6FSWEY4 [referral link]
- Memrise App: https://www.memrise.com/
- Fun words with no translation: https://www.optilingo.com/blog/german/16-german-words-no-english-translation/

# THE GERMAN BOOK MARKET

# STATISTICS

Before we dive deeper into the German book market, a quick note about statistics: Take them with a pinch of salt. Depending on the source of the data, indie books and/or eBooks aren't always included. For example, the German National Library (Deutsche Nationalbibliothek) requires books published in Germany to send them a copy. This doesn't always happen for print-on-demand and ebooks, meaning if statisticians only rely on data from the German National Library, many indie books won't be part of their research.

I apologise in advance for the onslaught of numbers you're about to face. I'm a big fan of statistics, but I know not everyone shares that passion.

## RESOURCES

- Monthly newsletter (in German) about changes in the book market: https://www.boersenverein.de/

markt-daten/marktforschung/branchen-monitor-buch/

- Data and market news from the German Publishers and Booksellers Association, Börsenverein des Deutschen Buchhandels (in German): https://www.boersenverein.de/markt-daten/

- Statista: Statistics & facts about the German publishing industry: https://www.statista.com/topics/6686/the-publishing-industry-in-germany/ (some free information, more behind a paywall)

- Study: What do Germans read (in German): https://www.splendid-research.com/de/studie-buecher.html

- News about the German publishing market by Publishing Perspectives: https://publishingperspectives.com/tag/germany/

**2**

# READING HABITS

In 2017, Splendid Research did a study about the reading habits of German adults. Careful, lots of numbers incoming.

- 61% of Germans read books regularly, 22% read every day, only 13% don't read at all
- 91% read print books, 41% ebooks and 24% listen to audiobooks.
- 49% only read print books, 6.5% only read ebooks.
- The three most popular genres are crime (50%), thrillers and non-fiction
- Split by gender, women prefer romance (34%) and historical fiction, men non-fiction about science and technology (36%) as well as science fiction. Women generally read more books than men.
- Parents spend about €29/month on books. 24% of adults spend more than €30/month on books.
- 76% buy their books online, 67% at brick-and-mortar book shops. 28% use libraries.
- 66% find the book blurb the most important

criteria for choosing a book. About half rely on recommendations from friends/family. Only 6.5% buy books they saw in ads.

- From a different study: 82% of Germans who read eBooks own an e-Reader.

You can download the full results of the study from the Splendid Research website (in German): https://www.splendid-research.com/de/studie-buecher.html

## 3

# SALES BY RETAILER

In 2019, almost half of Germany's book sales happened at traditional brick-and-mortar book shops. Internet sales were only one fifth - while that has gone up to a quarter during the Coronavirus pandemic, it's a comparatively small slice of the pie.

There are about 4,700 brick-and-mortar book shops in Germany, 90% of them small independent retailers. About a third of book shops have their own online store.

In addition, books are sold in another 1,300 other places like at supermarkets and petrol stations, which make up about 10% of all book sales (yes, Germans like to buy books wherever they are).

The remaining fifth are publishers selling direct to customers, industry and institutions (e.g. text books for schools).

Adult fiction makes up just under a third of book sales, while books for children and young adults were 17.2% of the book market in 2019.

## EBOOKS

In contrast to the US and UK book market, Amazon doesn't have as much of the pie in Germany. While it's difficult to find actual numbers (Amazon isn't very keen on sharing those), it's estimated that the Amazon share is around 45 to 55 percent. In self-publishing, it's likely to be higher, but again, it's not like the Zon offers to tell us.

The biggest competitor to Amazon for eBooks is tolino (yes, they use lower case for their brand), an alliance between the five biggest German book retailers as well as over 1,500 independent book shops. In 2019, tolino announced that they now own more than 40 percent of the German eBook market.

Google Play and Apple Books plus some smaller retailers make up the rest of the pie.

In my survey, Amazon and the tolino retailers were the platforms people had the most sales at, matching these statistics.

## PRINT BOOKS

It's a similar picture on the print market. Half of all online print book sale happen at brick-and-mortar book shops (which would compare to tolino's 40% share of the eBook market). Thalia is the most popular of them with a turnover of €1.2 billion in 2019.

When looking at online sales, less than half happen at Amazon. Self-publishing platform Tredition even suggests that only a quarter of online print book sales are done at Amazon.

# PRINT VS EBOOK

Print books still have a very important role in Germany. In fact, way more people read print books than eBooks, which is why I always recommend to have a print version of your book available.

Almost all of the authors I polled had print books or were planning to do so.

A big reason for this love of print books is *where* Germans buy their books. Bookshops at train stations and airports are extremely popular, and you can even get books at petrol stations and in supermarkets.

Among EU member states, Germany is the largest producer of print books. Worldwide, Germany makes up 9% of the publishing market (in terms of total sales).

In financial terms, eBooks only make up 6% of the book market's balance sheet. Yes, the picture is different for indie authors who don't have their books stocked and displayed in brick-and-mortar book shops like traditional publishers, but you should still take note of the eBook vs print book divide.

## TEENAGERS

Between 2008 and 2018, there was almost no change in how many teenagers regularly (several times a week) read print books: 40%, despite the growth of social media and eBooks. Only 16% of German teenagers never read a book in their free time.

In stark contrast to that, only 7% of teenagers read eBooks several times a week (data from 2018), a quarter of 12 to 19-year-olds read an eBook occasionally.

This shows that if you write books for young adults, you'll most definitely want to have print books available.

## ADULTS

For adults, it's a slightly different picture. During the coronavirus pandemic, eBook readers rose from a quarter to a third of the German adult population. This rises to more than half when looking at young people between 16 and 29. Still, that doesn't mean that they're reading less print books: eight out of ten Germans read print books at least occasionally.

There's hope for more eBook readers though: a third of those Germans who only read print books just now can imagine buying an eBook in the future.

## RESOURCES

- Lesen in Deutschland - study about young people's reading behaviour (in German): https://www.lesen-in-deutschland.de/html/content.php?object=journal&lid=1565
- Bi-yearly report on the German eBook market (in German): https://www.boersenverein.de/markt-daten/marktforschung/e-books/
- Article about changing reading habits during the corona virus pandemic (in German): https://www.bitkom.org/Presse/Presseinformation/In-der-Corona-Krise-greifen-mehr-Menschen-zum-E-Book

# 5

## INDIE AUTHOR SURVEY

Every year, Matthias Matting from the Selfpublisher Bibel, the most popular German self-publishing blog, conducts a survey with indie authors.

In 2020, almost 2000 authors completed his survey, which at first glance looks like a great number until you look at the demographics of those who took part. Over half earn less than €50/month and about a quarter have only published one book so far. Only 7% earn more than €2k/month, so be aware of that when taking in the results.

Let's have a look at two average successful German indie authors (those earning more than €2k/month). We shall call them Petra and Peter.

**Petra** publishes all her books as eBooks and three quarters of them as paperbacks. She doesn't usually bother with hardcovers. She's in KDP Select and makes over half of her income with page reads. 12% of her income is from paperbacks and 8.5% from audiobooks. She spends around €500/month on Amazon ads.

**Peter** decided to be wide and earns a third of his royalties at the tolino shops. His non-fiction print books are his main source of income. His favourite marketing strategies are social media (Facebook and Instagram in particular), his website and mouth-to-mouth recommendations.

---

## RESOURCES

Survey Part 1: https://www.selfpublisherbibel.de/selfpublishing-umfrage-2020-die-auswertung-teil-1-hobby-vs-professionalisierung/

Survey Part 2: https://www.selfpublisherbibel.de/selfpublishing-umfrage-2020-die-auswertung-teil-2-veroeffentlichungsstrategien/

Survey Part 3: https://www.selfpublisherbibel.de/selfpublishing-umfrage-2020-die-auswertung-teil-3-vermarktung-rezensionen-outsourcing/

# 6

# BESTSELLER LISTS

Many successful English-speaking authors will have a bestseller title like USA Today or New York Times Bestselling Author, but what equivalents are there in Germany?

First of all, when you look at German book covers you'll notice quickly that most of them don't have bestseller tags above the author name. Very occasionally, you'll find a badge or sticker pronouncing that the book is a bestseller, but even the most successful authors won't have a generic tag not specific to a particular book.

Some authors will mention their bestseller achievements in their bio or in book blurbs, but in general, bestseller tags aren't seen as important as in the English-speaking markets.

I did a little experiment and looked at the Top 50 Indie books on Thalia. Only one has a bestseller tag above the author's name (she's an American author using an USAT tag). Three have a BILD Bestseller badge and ten have a tolino Bestseller label.

(The tolino alliance has a joint bestseller list which combines eBook sales data from all their participating retailers: https://mytolino.de/tolino-bestseller/.)

All that said, you should still be aware of the main bestseller lists in Germany.

## 1. SPIEGEL

Der SPIEGEL is a weekly news magazine based in Hamburg and has been publishing book bestseller lists since 1961. Every Monday, they use sales data from over 9,000 book retailers in Germany, Austria and Switzerland (including online shops) to sort books by sales. They don't count eBooks towards sales.

The list is split by genre (fiction, non-fiction, advice/self-development, children/YA) with sub-categories for each of these (e.g. both fiction and non-fiction are split into hardcovers, paperbacks, trade paperbacks and audiobooks; while advice/self-development is split into life & health, food & drink, nature & garden, hobby & creativity). There's also a category for DVDs.

They have strict criteria for what books are allowed in which category. For example, paperbacks have to be at least 20.5cm high, otherwise they count as trade paperback. Advice/self-development books need to have a minimum price of €8.

## 2. BILD

BILD is Germany's - and indeed Europe's - most popular tabloid newspaper. In co-operation with Amazon they publish a weekly (sales from Sunday to Saturday) bestseller list based on Amazon.de sales only. Split into fiction and non-fiction, the list takes eBook, paperback and hardcover sales into consideration, as well as Kindle Unlimited borrows and other Amazon programmes like Prime Reading. Audiobooks don't count towards ranking.

Fiction bestsellers include the following categories: Contemporary fiction, Mystery/Thriller, Erotica, Fantasy and Science Fiction, Young Adult, Comics and Mangas.

Non-fiction bestsellers are taken from these categories: Biographies & Memoirs, Stock Exchange & Money, Business & Career, Computers, Film, Leisure, Home & Garden, Gift Books, Art & Culture, Cookery/Recipe Books, Science & Technology, Politics & History, Guidebooks, Travel, Religion & Spirituality, Sport.

## 3. BÖRSENBLATT

This both weekly and monthly bestseller list is curated by the German Publishers and Booksellers Association's trade magazine. They have eight categories: Fiction, Non-fiction, Children and Young Adult, Crime, Audiobooks, eBooks, Self-help, Independent. The latter is for books by independent publishers rather than self-publishers. Some of the main categories are then further divided into hardcover, paperback, trade paperback, and 'fast-climbing hardcovers'.

Just like the SPIEGEL list, they have minimum pricing requirements (€2.60 for eBooks, €5 for trade paperbacks, €8 for hardcovers and paperbacks).

They draw on sales data from over 6,500 book retailers (including online sales) and other shops where books are sold. They include sales data from Amazon but not Kindle Unlimited borrows.

## RESOURCES

- SPIEGEL bestseller list: https://www.spiegel.de/
  kultur/bestseller-buecher-belletristik-sachbuch-auf-
  spiegel-liste-a-458623.html
- SPIEGEL bestseller criteria & requirements:
  https://www.buchreport.de/spiegel-bestseller/
  ermittlung-der-bestseller/
- BILD bestseller list: https://www.bild.de/lifestyle/
  kultur/kultur/top-20-belletristik-und-sachbuecher-
  64566908.bild.html#fromWall
- Börsenblatt bestseller list: https://www.
  boersenblatt.net/aktuelle-boersenblatt-
  bestsellerliste-belletristik-bestseller-hardcover

# TRANSLATION

## 1

# WHICH BOOK TO TRANSLATE

If you are considering translations, you're likely in an advanced stage in your career and have multiple books and series. If you don't, it's easy, but if you do have a large backlist, you'll have to decide on which book to start with. Your bestselling series might not necessarily be the best choice, so I recommend the following steps to come to an informed decision:

1. Take a look at which of your books already sell well in Germany, Austria and Switzerland (if you're exclusive to Amazon, you'll only be able to look at Germany). This will give you an indication of what readers there enjoy - although be aware that sales might be coming from expats, so take this with a grain of salt.
2. Look at retailer bestseller lists. Here it's important to not just look at Amazon.de (be sure to set the book language to 'German'), but also the other main German book retailers like Thalia,

buecher.de and Hugendubel. Bonus points if you also utilise Apple Books and Google Books.

3. Thalia has a page specifically for self-published books which can be a great resource: https://www.thalia.de/kategorie/self-publishing-16891/

4. If you only look at the Amazon bestseller lists, thanks to Amazon's ranking algorithms most of the books you'll see will be in KDP Select/Kindle Unlimited. Books that aren't in KU will have lower ranks even if they sell just as many copies or even more. Even if you plan to be in KDP Select, it's still worth researching books that aren't.

5. When doing research on retailer sites, you'll want to be in incognito mode and not logged in with your account - you don't want your past searches to influence the results. Even better, use a German proxy server so it looks as if you're browsing from Germany.

6. Read through official bestseller lists like those published by BILD and SPIEGEL.

7. Stalk other authors (or you could talk to them) in your genre. If you know an author writing similar books to your own has translations, check how well they're doing.

8. Research which genres might be under-served by traditional publishers. If you write romance, the contemporary and historical romance genres are heavily dominated by trad publishers. Of course, this means these genres are popular and full of hungry readers, but it also means that it's much harder to break into those genres and gain visibility. Unless you have a massive marketing budget, it might be wiser to focus on genres that aren't served by traditional publishers. Sticking

with romance, that would be paranormal and sci-fi romance, especially the steamier variety.

9. Evergreen vs current trends. If you write to market and focus on the latest trends, you will discover that those trends don't always translate into foreign markets. Using another romance example, 'bully romance' may be popular just now with English-speaking readers, while it's unheard of in Germany.

10. Since translations can take several months to complete - and if you have a longer series, it could therefore be a year or longer until your series is complete in German - I generally advise to stick with evergreen themes that will still appeal to a wide audience in several years' time.

> "I started with my series that was one of the shortest (so less expensive to do the whole thing) and evergreen tropes (shifters, fated mates). From there I'm going for a mix of how popular the books have been and how many popular tropes they have."
>
> — ANONYMOUS

**Resources**

Indie published books at Thalia: https://www.thalia.de/kategorie/self-publishing-16891/

## 2

# FINDING A TRANSLATOR

Now that you've decided which book/series you'll want to get translated, one of the hardest parts of the process begins: finding a translator.

Not all translators are the same and not all of them will be the right people for your book. You'll want a *literary* translator who specialises in translating *books*, not medical reports, not marriage certificates, not court transcripts. Just knowing the vocabulary, grammar and method of translating isn't enough.

Literary translators are writers. They don't just translate word by word. They know how to convey emotion, give characters a distinct voice, work with rhythm and style. They make the text flow, choosing the perfect words that sound right and give meaning. Give two translators the same source text and you'll end up with two different books, each with their own tone and voice.

I like to compare it to having a book read by a professional narrator versus a text-to-speech programme. The latter will be convey the text correctly (with a few mispronunciations), but do you really want to listen to an entire book read by Alexa? A human narrator will add emotion, different accents and voices, pace and pauses, turning the text into an experience.

It's the same for translations and why it's so important to find the right translator.

> "I had one translator who translated literal direct instead of letting the language flow - hence I had to get it re-edited. Stick to people who live in Germany, not someone who speaks German in another country."
>
> — MILA YOUNG

## WORD OF MOUTH

The easiest way for sure is to ask other authors for recommendations. 40% of the authors I polled found their translators this way.

You can also browse translated books on retailers and, after checking that they don't have any mentions of bad translations in the reviews, look at the copyright page to find the translator.

*[Personal plea: Please always credit your translator. As said above, they're writers/artists in their own right. They will pour a lot of heart blood into the translation. They deserve to be credited.]*

The problem with this strategy is that many authors are very protective of their translators and aren't always willing to share. Since translations take quite a while, an author with multiple books could easily book a translator for an entire year.

---

## TRANSLATOR ASSOCIATION

An easy way to find a large number of translators is to use the membership databases of German translator associations. Their members are usually vetted and require to have gone through professional training, so you can be sure that you'll end up with a translator who knows what they're doing.

There are two big associations I recommend to look at: The VDÜ and the BDÜ. The VDÜ specialises in literary translations while the BDÜ is for translators in general.

- VDÜ – Verband deutschsprachiger Übersetzer literarischer und wissenschaftlicher Werke e.V = National association for German translators of literary & scientific works
- They have an online database of over 850 translators: https://literaturuebersetzer.de/uevz.
- While their website is in German, simply enter 'Englisch' in the search field and you'll see over 600 translators. You can refine the search by using terms from their list which includes genres and non-fiction subjects.

- BDÜ – Berufsverband professioneller Dolmetscher und Übersetzer in Deutschland
- They have a membership database in English: https://search.bdue.de/.

---

## FREELANCER DATABASES

A third of the authors I spoke to found their translators on freelancer sites like Upwork and Fiverr. One specifically for language professionals is ProZ

Vetting is especially important for translators you find on freelance sites (see next chapter). Be wary of those charging rock-bottom prices, there's usually a reason for that.

**Language Professionals:**

- https://www.proz.com/
- https://www.translatorscafe.com/
- https://www.translatorsbase.com/
- https://www.selfpublishingmarkt.de/listing-category/uebersetzung/

**General Freelancers:**

- https://www.upwork.com/
- https://www.peopleperhour.com/
- https://www.fiverr.com/

---

## REEDSY

You may know Reedsy as a free formatting tool, but they also have a marketplace for publishing professionals. They have a strict vetting system which means they only accept about 5% of applicants, which means you'll definitely end up with an experienced translator who knows their craft.

At the time of writing, they have about twenty German translators to choose from. You simply set up a project on their platform and can then invite translators to make you an offer.

The average cost varies and depends on the level of involvement of the translator: i.e. whether they'll do editing/proofreading passes afterwards (or outsource them to a colleague), help with marketing materials, etc. That said, most quotes on Reedsy are in the €0.08-€0.12 per word range.

They charge a 10% fee on top of the translator's rate.

https://reedsy.com/translation/book-translator

(or use my referral link to get $25 credit: https://reedsy.com/r/skye-mackinnon)

By the way, Reedsy also have an excellent free course on international book pricing:

https://blog.reedsy.com/learning/courses/distribution/pricing-books-international/

> German is definitely the #1 language to start with if you're looking to expand to other

markets. If you're a high-selling author, you probably already have some readers on your mailing list/reader group who live in Germany, so you should try to leverage their help at launch (beta reading, reviews, word of mouth, etc.).

— RICARDO FAYET, REEDSY

## TRANSLATION AGENCIES

There are many agencies employing a number of translators. They'll match you with one and will usually handle all the paperwork, payments etc. Using an agency can make it harder to vet the individual translator since you won't always be able to choose who you'll be matched with.

One such agency is the Libelli Agentur, which has been recommended to me by several authors: http://www.libelliagency.com/

## REVENUE SHARE PLATFORMS

There are two platforms that will offer you to go into a royalty-share agreement with a translator, therefore making this the cheapest (but not necessarily best) option: Babelcube and Tektime. The disadvantage with both of these is that you give up a lot of control. You can't decide where you publish your books, you can't go into KDP

Select, you can't access retailer promotions, you're bound to them for five years.

Let's have a closer look at them.

# 3

## BABELCUBE

B abelcube describes itself as a 'platform to bring self-published authors and publishers together with freelance translators to create books in additional languages and sell them around the world.'

If you see translations as a chance for a passive income, this is the most passive way of all, the one where you lie on your hammock with a cocktail and let others do the leg work for you. Translation, distribution, payments and sales reporting are all done via the same platform.

They have a staggered revenue split that becomes more favourable for the author with increasing sales. For the first $2,000 of net sales, the author receives 30% which then increases to 45% ($2k - $5k), 65% ($5k to $8k) and culminates at 75% for all net sales over $8k. Babelcube takes a 20% cut. This means that for a book that makes $8,000, the translator ends up with only $2,500, which is a lot less than most professional translators would charge.

Babelcube distributes ebooks (but not paperbacks) wide, i.e. to multiple retailers, not just Amazon. That way you can reach 300+ retailers and 20,000 libraries. Your book won't be in Kindle Unlimited, which can either be good or bad depending on your publishing strategy.

You retain the rights to the translated book, but Babel has the distribution rights for five years. After this period, the rights revert to you.

**The good:**

- This is the cheapest way to get your book translated because there's no upfront cost.
- They distribute both the ebook and paperback for you, saving time and effort.
- Saves you from having to search for a translator.
- Translators can team up with other translators or editors to offer you their services as a package deal.
- You get a free sample translation before you decide whether to continue with the project or not.

**The bad** (all based on comments from authors and translators who've used the platform):

- Very few (potentially none at all) professional translators are willing to work for just royalty share and no upfront payment. The translators you'll find on Babelcube are often inexperienced and untrained.
- Translations can be very hit and miss. Most authors

report of at least one instance where the translation was unusable and clearly machine-translated.

- Paperbacks are published only on Amazon.
- The publication process can be slow and edits take a while to appear in published books.
- Sometimes translators seem to disappear after agreeing to do a project.
- If you're outside the US and your country doesn't have a tax treaty with the US, Babelcube will withhold 30% of your royalties.
- Babelcube won't do any marketing for you and there's no guarantee that your translator will, either.

---

## RESOURCES

Babelcube: https://www.babelcube.com

# TEKTIME

Tektime is very similar to Babelcube with a few distinct differences:

- They also offer audiobook translations & narration.
- There's an option for the author to offer a 'translation grant', an upfront fee aimed at attracting the best translators. The author pays the fee after approving a sample, but the translator won't receive it until the translation is complete.
- The author's share starts at 15% for the first $1,000 in net sales and is capped at 80% for sales over $8k (compared to 30% and 75% at Babelcube).
- Their fee is 10% compared to Babelcube's 20%.
- They have volunteer readers to assess the quality of the translation, authors pay a €10 'tip' for this.
- They can run Amazon advertising campaigns for you, taking yet more work off you.
- Tektime has their own online store, although it seems to be selling mostly Italian-language books.

Just like with Babelcube, the contract is for five years, after which you can do with your translation as you wish.

Their platform feels a little old-fashioned and not always intuitive. After registering, you set up an entry for your book with the possibility of adding sales data (you'll want to show translators that it's worth putting effort into this book). You can also choose whether to offer a translation grant or not.

You can then either wait for translators to contact you or you can be proactive and send a proposal to them. You're able to see ratings for previous translations and feedback from authors. On the translator profile pages you can also check if they're currently working on other translations and when they're due - that will give you an idea of their availability.

One negative point I found mentioned several time is that because Tektime is based in Italy, there's a withholding tax for everyone not resident in Italy. While with Babelcube - if your country has a tax treaty with the US - you can get them to stop withholding the tax by filling in a form, with Tektime you have to deal with the Italian Revenue Agency yourself to get a tax refund.

## RESOURCES

- Tektime (affiliate link)
- Tektime book store

# 5

# TEKTIME CASE STUDY

## AN AUTHOR'S PERSPECTIVE BY L.G. CASTILLO

Some authors may be concerned about verifying that a translation is good when not knowing the language. There may be fear of publishing a poorly translated book. Because I viewed this as an experiment and learning process, I was okay if my translated books were not perfect. I looked forward to reader reviews to tell me the quality of the translations.

So far, readers love the translations. I may have had one or two complaints about a word or two used in a translation.

I interview most of the translators. I talk with some via Skype. I get their email and/or Facebook information so that I can message them outside of Tektime. And I invite them to contact me at any time if they have questions about the books.

Tektime offers a service where a reader (a native speaker) reads the book and evaluates the translation. The reader gets a discount on the Tektime bookstore in return.

Tektime also offers Amazon advertising. I do ads myself, so I don't use this service.

Here is the downside of working with Tektime. They are an Italian based company working abiding by Italian law. So when they pay me, they withhold 30% as required by Italian law. They provide information on how to apply to the Italian Revenue Agency for a tax refund. This may be a deal breaker for authors.

Tektime has wonderful support. I always get a response to my emails within hours. My books show up for sale on Amazon within 24 hours and other retailers within 48 hours.

**L.G. Castillo, author of the Reign of Angels Series**

## 6

# VETTING YOUR TRANSLATOR

Once you've found a few translators you're considering for the job, it's time to put on your recruitment consultant hat and vet the candidates. Almost half of the respondents to my survey said they had a bad experience with translators, with most of them saying they wish they'd chosen someone else.

> "I wasn't sure if my normal translator would have time to translate the blurbs for my books, so I hired someone just for my blurbs. A German speaking author reached out to me and let me know the blurbs were horribly translated, so I got rid of them, and just hired my original translator to redo them. It was a lesson, for sure."
>
> — LACEY CARTER ANDERSEN

Don't be afraid to ask lots of questions.

1. How much experience do they have with literary translations, specifically in your genre? Don't just take their word for it, search for them at retailers and read through reviews.

2. What are their qualifications? Do they have a degree or other formal training in translation? Do they specialise in literary translations?

3. Are they comfortable with translating things like steamy scenes, violence, etc?

4. Are they a native speaker?

5. Where do they live? If they're in Germany or another German-speaking country, you'll have to be aware of the copyright laws and other legalities of their country (more on that later). If they live in an English-speaking country, how long have they lived there? I can tell you from my own experience that after living in Scotland for over a decade, my German grammar is not what it used to be and I'm not up to date with many colloquialisms. If I had to choose, I'd always employ a German native speaker living in a German-speaking country.

6. Who will own the copyright?

7. Will they deliver an edited, proofread translation or will you have to find your own editor/proofreader? Do they have contacts they can share to help you find proofreaders and/or beta readers?

8. Will they translate your blurbs, bio, website, etc? Can they help with marketing materials and social media posts? Will they promote your book on their platform?

9. How long will it take them to translate your book? If they tell you anything under 3-4 weeks, be wary.

Translating a book can take longer than writing it in the first place.

10. What's their availability like? If you have a large backlist, mention that right away. You'll want to get your whole series done by the same translator and won't want to end up having to wait for months to get a sequel translated.

11. Do they offer a sample translation?

12. Can they provide samples of their previous translations?

13. How are you going to communicate? Emails only or will there be Skype/Zoom calls to discuss the book and any questions that might arise?

14. And of course, what do they charge? Is their price based on the word/page count of the original book or the translation? Do they want a deposit? Do they offer a payment plan? Do they want a share of the royalties (very common in Germany)?

You'll probably be able to come up with even more questions specific to your situation. Don't be shy, ask them all. You don't want to find out halfway through the translation process that there has been some sort of misunderstanding.

> "Audition your translators and get several opinions on their work from at least three German editors."

— ADDISON CAIN

One important part of the vetting process is getting a sample translation. This doesn't have to be the beginning of your book; choose a scene that showcases your style. If you write romance, it can be a good idea to give them a steamy scene to see if they can handle those. Find a native speaker to look over the sample to determine if it's any good. If you don't have friends who speak German, ask in your reader groups, your social networks or hire a freelancer. Some authors will also use this sample process to at the same time vet proof readers - give the same sample to several proofreaders and see if they'll all highlight the same things.

While some translators will charge for a sample, many will do it for free.

## RESOURCES

*Indie Translations* offer paid evaluations of translation samples: https://indie-translations.com/news/

# 7

# IS MACHINE TRANSLATION ANY GOOD?

Should you ever (or can you ever) use AI like DeepL to translate into German?

Not if you don't have a native speaker to look over it.

One of my favourite examples as a romance author is 'steamy'. If you enter the term 'steamy romance' into DeepL, you're given 'dampfige Romanze' as a result. You do not want to use that in a blurb or in a social media post. 'Dampfig' means steamy in the context of cooking, of boiling water. It has nothing to do with sexy.

This little example shows how important it is to always have someone check even the smallest pieces of text. No matter how good your book is, if a reader sees you use something like 'dampfende Romanze' in a Facebook post, they will assume your book translation is just as bad.

But what about Joanna Penn, I hear you ask. If you've looked into human vs machine translation before, you'll probably have come across her experiment back in 2019. Joanna translated several of her non-fiction books by throwing them into DeepL before employing a team of editors and translators to turn them into readable books. The advantage of doing this is that when using DeepL, the copyright stays with the author (more on the copyright issue in the next chapter).

While the initial translation was much cheaper than employing a human translator, it still cost her a lot for editing, formatting, marketing and of course her time in dealing with all those people. She says it took both more money and more time than she'd expected.

While this is an interesting way of translating non-fiction books, I don't believe the same would work for fiction for all the reasons we already discussed.

---

Joanna Penn has written a great summary of her experiences: https://www.thecreativepenn.com/2019/11/22/self-publishing-german-ai/

# 8

# WHY YOU SHOULD USE A REAL HUMAN

## A TRANSLATOR'S VIEW BY ANNETTE KURZ

There is no doubt that machine translation, starting with Google Translate in 2006 and followed by programs like Linguee and DeepL have had a huge impact on the industry. The results are getting better almost by the day; Neural Machine Translation even tries to imitate our brains and has moved on from mere rules-based linguistic translation to including context and learning how to recognise phrases. AI is beginning to learn at multiple levels, has enormous corpora at its disposal and is faster than humans. And it's cheap in comparison – so what's not to like?

Let's start by looking at what we do when we translate a text, in our case a literary work of fiction. We transfer it from a source language (SL) to the target language (TL) observing structural rules (syntax) and meanings of words and phrases (semantics). However, this is only the tip of the iceberg – **meaning** is what we are after, the text in TL should have the same effect on a reader of this language as the original had on readers in SL. Ideally, the translation reproduces the experience of reading the original and you should be able to read it like an original in TL without stumbling over uncommon or even incomprehensible expressions. Add to this beauty, subtlety, innuendo, cultural allusions, language rhythm, to name only the most obvious, and you realise how complex the undertaking really is.

I'm a German native speaker and have met with quite a few challenges when translating some of Skye MacKinnons' books. At the semantic level, a recurring problem is that in many cases there is no *one to one word equivalence*, e.g. the English "mate" would have a number of possible translations depending on the context. *Gender* is a big issue, there being three grammatical genders in German (masculine, feminine, neuter) irrespective of natural gender. So in order to make the text in TL unambiguous it is often necessary to use nouns / names more often than pronouns. Idioms and metaphors do not always have an equivalent in TL: In a children's book that I've recently translated, "the blue whale is feeling blue". The first "blue" (belonging to this particular species of whales) is the same as in German, the second one not at all since it refers to an emotional state. However, DeepL translates "Der Blauwal fühlt sich blau" leaving the German reader totally at a loss.

*Telling names* can be another hurdle – or are they "telling" at all? If it is not extremely obvious (as in cats' names like Biter or Taillie), best ask the author themselves. And this is a definite advantage the human translator has: They will recognise when a little *chinwag* – or should I say *consultation / talk / discussion* (the choice is a matter of *register* or *level of formality*, another consideration when doing the job properly) with the author of the original is important. What was their intention in this particular case?

In an ideal world, the translator cooperates with the author.

And yes, contracting with human translators costs money. Unfortunately, the title "translator" is not legally protected (at least here in Germany), so anyone with some language knowledge may use it. It's therefore useful to find out about the individual's experience and education – the most trustworthy institutions that provide the latter are Universities and Universities of Applied Sciences ("Hochschule") where you graduate with a BA or MA or – before the introduction of these international degrees – with a diploma after a four-year course of studies. You can also take an exam at the Chambers of Industry and Commerce ("Industrie- und Handelskammern") and call yourself "certified translator" (not to be confused with the "publicly appointed translator"/interpreter who works for the regional courts and is sworn in, also often called "certified") but this is in no way comparable to the university degree either in course content (geared towards the demands of industry and commerce, as the name would suggest) or duration.

So in the best case, a highly qualified language expert will do your translation.

Regarding pricing, it's worth noting that the German translation will always be longer than the original in English. This is not because the translator wants to make more money (in Germany payment is often by standard line/word in TL, not of the original in SL!) but down to the idiosyncrasies of either language. Structures like gerunds or certain participle constructions that make English rather more concise do simply not exist in German, where they need to be replaced by a clause or a whole new sentence – remember, we translate *meaning*, not words.

Which brings us back to why we are doing this in the first place... Especially in literary texts, there are often second and third levels of meaning (just think of the vast area of shared cultural/historical background in any language community), novel usages of language and/or sounds (e.g. rhymes, alliterations, love of certain structures because they have a certain rhythm) which may render some sentences or parts thereof untranslatable in the narrow sense of the word. In the wider, a good (human) translator will look for an approximation and try to at least get close to the intended meaning and function of this word/phrase/sentence within its context.

It should be obvious that in light of the complexity of literary language and the required flexibility when translating it human management is still required. Software programs are useful tools and can possibly increase the productivity of a human translator – but careful, in-depth editing of sentence structure, style and language register on top of simple elimination of spelling errors (never trust your spell check!) and grammar mistakes by such a human professional are an absolute must for good results when using machine translation.

**Annette Kurz, certified translator for German, English and Spanish**

## 9

# THE COST OF TRANSLATIONS

Like in all aspects of self-publishing, the price of translations varies wildly, although you can usually expect to pay several thousand Euros for a book translation.

Traditionally, cost is calculated by 'Normseite', a standard page. One page has 1,500 characters: 30 lines with 50 characters each. Some translators who're used to working with indie authors now set their prices per word, but you will still find many who calculate their prices by Normseite.

The VDÜ literary translator association recommends a minimum of €19 per Normseite (€23 for particularly difficult translations) plus a share of royalties: 1% for print books, 1.6% for audiobooks and 2.5% for eBooks and other digital versions.

Considering a Normseite is around 250 words, that would give us a rate of €0.076 per word.

This royalty share is something that surprises and shocks many authors who aren't used to providing royalties to service providers. It stems from the fact that the law sees the translator as the *author* of the translation, which makes them eligible for royalties from the publisher just like the author of the original book. Since indie publishing is still relatively new in Germany (and translating self-published books even more so), translators are used to the contracts offered by traditional publishers which offer a royalty share. Both Draft2Digital and Feiyr offer a royalty split feature that automatically pays your translator if you agree to a royalty share with them.

You will find translators charging less and charging more than the rate recommended by the VDÜ. In my little survey, the lowest was €0.03/word, but most were in the range of €0.06-0.08/word. Professional literary translators with lots of experience will rarely charge less than €0.10. On Reedsy, standard rates are between €0.08 and €0.12.

If you write poetry or children's books in rhyme, you will likely have to pay a premium. I had one rhymed picture book translated and my translator said it was one of the hardest projects she's worked on even though the book was only 32 pages long.

Small warning, some translators will charge additional VAT (19% on translations). Make sure to ask about that when getting a quote.

Be aware that some translation rates might look very cheap but don't include editing or proofreading. Proof reading starts around €2/Normseite and expect good copy-editing to cost at least €4/Normseite.

As a side note, according to section 32 of the all-important 'Act on Copyright and Related Rights'

(Urheberrechtsgesetz), your translator has the right to 'equitable remuneration'. While this is quite vague, remember that the translator will spend as least as long on the translation as you spent writing the book in the first place.

If it makes you feel better about the high cost of translations, everyone in my survey said they broke even within the first year. 40% even broke even within the first month! (that deserves an exclamation mark)

Three quarters of them also made five figures or more from their German translations (2020, in USD).

---

## RESOURCES

Act on Copyright and Related Rights in English: https:// www.gesetze-im-internet.de/ englisch_urhg/englisch_urhg.html

# CONTRACT

Having a contract is one of the most important parts of the entire translation process. In fact, without it, you'd be unable to publish your translation according to German law (more on that later).

If your translator is experienced, they will provide the contract. If the contract is in German, ask for a copy translated into English.

It's advisable to have your contract vetted by a legal professional. Several author associations like the Society of Authors offer free contract vetting to their members (I used them for my own translation contract and they couldn't have been more helpful).

**What should definitely be mentioned in your contract:**

  1. Name of your book, your legal name and your pen

name, the translator's name (and their pen name if they use one for certain genres)

2. Scope of the work - number of words or standard pages; any additional translations like your bio, blurbs, social media posts, etc

3. Time frame - deadlines for you to deliver the manuscript and for the translator to deliver the translation

4. Rights - the translator grants you the exploitation rights (Nutzungsrechte) of the translation with no geographic or time restrictions. Mention explicitly what formats of the translation you're planning to publish (eBook, audiobook, etc). The translator has the right to be named in the book and on the product page at retailers.

5. Other rights - what happens when you use the translation to produce audiobooks etc. Will the translator get royalties?

6. Compensation - what you pay the translator, potential royalties they'll receive, deposits, payment plans. How will they be paid?

7. Problem resolution - what happens if the translator doesn't deliver or delivers a bad translation? What happens if you don't pay on time? Which country's laws apply?

Personally, I'd also include a paragraph confirming that your translator will do the translation personally and without the help of AI or sub-contractors. I've heard some horror stories from authors who eventually realised that their translator had outsourced the work to freelancers on Fiverr.

## RESOURCES

- Sample contract by the VDÜ (in German): https://
  literaturuebersetzer.de/berufspraktisches/
  rechtliches/normvertrag/
- Sample contract by Literaturhaus Wien (pdf; in
  German): http://www.literaturhaus.at/fileadmin/
  user_upload/autorInnen/pdf/ueg/Mustervertrag.pdf

## COPYRIGHT

A s I've already mentioned, according to German law, the copyright of the translation lies with the translator. This is because they're seen as an author in their own right.

> "Copyright is based on the idea of originality: any new expression that is different from existing expressions, is considered the inalienable intellectual property of its author and, as such, enjoys automatic protection. Just like musical or dramatic performances, literary translations are in a double copyright situation: on the one hand there is the copyright of the original author, and on the other the copyright of the translator, who is the author of this particular translation, as distinct from all other possible translations of the same text. This is why the translator enjoys exactly the same legal rights as a writer. It also means that literary translation is not just work for hire, but a form

of free expression: when signing a contract with a translator, a publisher is actually commissioning an original work that bears the stamp of its author."

— EUROPEAN COUNCIL OF LITERARY
TRANSLATORS' ASSOCIATIONS
(HTTPS://WWW.CEATL.EU/TRANSLATORS-
RIGHTS/LEGAL-STATUS)

Copyright cannot be transferred to you, but the translator can transfer the exploitation rights (Nutzungsrechte) to you with a contract, giving you full authority to publish the book. As long as you credit the translator, you'll be able to do with the translation whatever you wish (as set out in your contract). However, if you don't have a contract, you technically won't be able to do anything with the translation (and neither will your translator) - so it's extremely important to have a proper contract from the get-go.

> A joint author may waive his share of the exploitation rights. He shall make a declaration of waiver to the other joint authors.

— ACT ON COPYRIGHT AND RELATED
RIGHTS, SECTION 8

## RESOURCES

Act on Copyright and Related Rights: https://www.gesetze-im-internet.de/englisch_urhg/englisch_urhg.html

# 12

# INTERVIEW WITH LAWYER ARNO LAMPMANN

A rno Lampmann, a German lawyer specialising in trade mark, competition, copyright and media law. He agreed to answer some questions relevant to self-publishers for this book.

## Do foreign authors who do not live in Germany have to include a postal address in the imprint?

Yes, the state press laws of the German federal states (e.g. the state press law of North Rhine-Westphalia in §8) stipulate that the name or company and address of the printer and the publisher, in the case of self-publishing of the author or the publisher, must be stated on every printed work published in their jurisdictional territory. The wording of the state press laws differs in some cases. Which law is relevant depends on the place of publication (not on where they are ultimately distributed).

. . .

## If an author is registered as a self-employed person or company abroad, is the town or city sufficient or must the full address be stated?

If there is a printer or publisher, only his or her name and address must be included. The author can then even publish under a pseudonym. If the author is self-published, his or her name and full address must also be stated.

## Are pen names permissible in the imprint?

Yes, but only if the author does not print or publish the book himself (see above).

## Are pseudonym or imprint services legal?

These services are not illegal. However, they are unsuitable for fulfilling the imprint requirement. Either the author has a printer or publisher. In that case, he does not have to give his details anyway. Or, if the author is self-published, he or she must also give his or her own address (for service of process). A third-party address is not sufficient in this case, as it must be ensured that legal action can actually be taken against the person responsible in the event of a dispute.

## What about imprints on websites?

The obligation to provide an imprint for websites is a topic of its own. It is determined by the German Telemedia Act (TMG), but also by the Interstate Broadcasting Services Agreement (Rundfunkstaatsvertrag) in the case of publication of journalistic content. There are numerous imprint generators on the internet that can be used to ensure that none of the required information is missing.

Anyone who publishes content that is not purely private is obliged to have an imprint. It must be accessible from every page. If journalistic content is also published, a separate person responsible for it must be stated (name and address, for example "Responsible for the content according to § 55 para. 2 RStV: Name, address".). This also applies to blog content, among other things.

**Is it legally stipulated that the author may only make changes to the translation with the translator's consent?**

The translator is granted his or her own copyright to the translation, which enables him or her to exclude third parties from using the work in principle. Even adaptations or other alterations of the work may only be published or used with the translator's consent. This even applies to the author himself. It is therefore very important that the author establishes with the translator exactly which rights he or she will later be entitled to regarding the translated text.

**Can a translator's copyright be inherited by his or her descendants?**

Copyright, and thus also that of the translator, can be inherited. However, it expires 70 years after the death of the author.

. . .

**Does the Copyright Act also apply to German translators who live abroad?**

Yes. German nationals enjoy copyright protection for all their works, regardless of whether and where the works were published.

**What do I do if someone uses my already published title?**

A distinctive title is protected as soon as the work appears, without the need for registration or any other formality. The right holder is thereby granted an exclusive right; this means that the owner of the title is granted, by law, an exclusive and sole right to use and exploit the title. A third party is prohibited from making unauthorised use of the title in the course of trade in a manner likely to cause confusion with the protected title.

**For what should one hire a (German) lawyer? Should every contract be checked by a lawyer?**

If a work is to be translated into German and also distributed in Germany, it is essential to seek the advice of an expert who is familiar with copyright law. Firstly, because it must be contractually agreed with the translator which rights of use the author has in the translation, secondly, which law applies and thirdly, which courts of which state should have jurisdiction in the event of a dispute.

**Thank you very much for the interview.**

. . .

*Arno Lampmann is a partner in the Cologn-based law firm Lampmann, Haberkamm & Rosenbaum (LHR). He is an author, mentor and expert in trade mark, competition, copyright and media law and, as a specialist in intellectual property law, supports international companies, artists and personalities in the fast and effective enforcement of their rights and the protection of their good reputation.*

*He has access to an international network of experts and contacts both in Germany and in the USA, particularly in the location of the most important internet companies, in the Bay Area and in Silicon Valley.*

*He is co-author of the Handbuchs Multimedia-Recht (Multimedia Law Handbook), edited by Professor Thomas Hoeren, among others, and at Recht Am Bild and Legal Tribune Online.*

You can contact him in English or German.

**Rechtsanwälte Lampmann, Haberkamm & Rosenbaum Partnerschaft**

Stadtwaldgürtel 81-83

50935 Köln

Tel 0221 2716733-0

Fax 0221 2716733-33

E-Mail: lampmann@lhr-law.de

https://www.lhr-law.de/en/kanzlei/team/a-lampmann/

## 13

# THE TRANSLATION PROCESS

The translation process is similar to writing a book. There will be drafts, edits, proofreads and beta reads. It can take several months, depending on the length of your book and the availability of your chosen translator.

Some translators will edit and proofread themselves, others will outsource it, others will expect you to deal with that. Be sure to confirm from the start what your translator is offering.

## DURING THE TRANSLATION

While you might think that all you do is to send your manuscript to your translator, this isn't always true for every project. Sometimes, your translator will have questions about things like translating names, acronyms, what you meant with that sentence, and more. There might also be the question of whether characters use the informal or formal you with each other. For example, in my Catnip

Assassins series, the first books I had translated, my main character is a killer for hire. She has important clients who you'd usually address with the formal 'Sie', but because she's a street rat with no manners and little respect for others, we decided that she's going to use the informal 'du' for everyone. In cases like that, it's good to have a chat with your translators and make a decision together.

## EDITING

Since your story won't have changed during translation, you likely won't need a Lektorat (developmental editing) but only a Korrektorat or Korrekturlesen (copy editing). However, if your translator is inexperienced or readers tell you that your book's style is wonky, you might want to consider a Lektorat after all.

Finding an experienced editor can be just as difficult as finding a translator. If your translator can't recommend anyone, try word of mouth, freelance sites or the database of the Verband der Freien Lektorinnen und Lektoren (VFLL), the association of self-employed editors: https://www.lektoren.de. You can also find a directory of editors (along with many other author service providers) on Selfpublishingmarkt.de.

Of the authors I polled, two thirds used a proofreader and/or an editor, although others had it included in the price of their translation.

## BETA READERS

You don't necessarily need beta readers ('Testleser') - for the same reason you don't need developmental editing - but

I've found them helpful not just for getting feedback on the story, but also for finding your first German fans and making connections.

You can try and ask around among your existing readers if there are any who speak German and would like to beta read, or try Facebook groups like 'Testleser gesucht' and 'Testleser gesucht! Autoren überarbeiten ihre Manuskripte!'. I've been told by the group admins that you can post beta reader requests in English.

## NEXT STEPS

Congratulations, the first part is done! Now that you have a polished translation, it's time to think of what other steps to take before you can share your book with readers. In the next section of this book we'll look at formatting, deciding on titles, covers, pricing and more.

## RESOURCES

- List of editors on Selfpublishingmarkt.de: https://www.selfpublishingmarkt.de/Inserate/?listing_category=korrektorat
- Facebook groups for beta readers: https://www.facebook.com/groups/1565769440339922 and https://www.facebook.com/groups/684104681650060

Selection of editors specialising in editing/proofreading translated texts:

- http://www.dualect.de/kontakt.php
- https://www.wortberatung.de/kontakt/
- https://www.lektorat-lloyd.de/kontakt/
- https://www.christinabrombach.com/

# PREPARING TO PUBLISH

## 1

# DECIDING ON A TITLE

A translation of your English title is of course the easiest, but not necessarily the best option. Different genres have different conventions, but here are a few general ideas.

### 1) One word title

Popular, can be very memorable, but very hard to find titles that haven't been used already.

### 2) Compound nouns

This is especially popular for romance and thrillers. By combining two nouns you're creating a new, poignant word which is likely unique.

Examples: 'Himbeermond' (raspberry moon), 'Blutkralle' (blood claw)

### 3) Say what's in the tin

Easy and effective. My favourite example: 'The Hundred-Year-Old Man Who Climbed Out the Window and Disappeared'

## 4) Combine a name with the action

The Harry Potter titles are a good example, e.g. 'Harry Potter and the Goblet of Fire'.

## 5) Play with metaphors and alliterations

You'll definitely need your translator to help with this one since metaphors and plays on words rarely are translatable.

## 6) Confusing titles

Titles that make the reader stop and think are popular particularly with non-fiction.

Examples: 'The 4-hour-week', 'Ein ganzes halbes Jahr' (= a whole half year).

## 7) Create an image

Give the reader an experience for all senses. 'Der Duft von Pinienkernen' (= the scent of pine nuts) or 'Fischbrötchen und Salzkaramell' (= fish sandwiches and salted caramel) are great examples for this.

## 8) Combine English and German

In romance especially, it's not uncommon to mix and match the two languages by using one language in the title and the other in the subtitle.

Examples: 'Paper Princess: Die Versuchung' or 'Blood and Ash - Liebe kennt keine Grenzen'. I did this with my most recent translation, turning the original 'Rescued by Bears' into 'Highland Shifters - Von Bären gerettet')

## 9) English only

It might surprise you to know that some German authors use English titles (and pseudonyms). An example would be 'Hearts on Fire' by Emily Bold (she's German).

## 10) Highlight the location

Germans love novels (and films) set in romantic and exotic locations. The British Isles are a particular favourite.

Examples: 'Die Nebel von Skye' (= the mists of Skye), 'Verliebt in Texas' (= in love in Texas)

Here's a great article about this phenomenon: https://www.theguardian.com/world/2021/may/29/german-tv-love-cornwall-diplomats-rosamunde-pilcher

Be aware that capitalisation in titles is different from the English convention. Only nouns are capitalised in titles.

## 2

## TITLE PROTECTION

The most important thing you need to be aware of when deciding on a title for your German translation is that German law requires every book to have a unique title (= Titelschutz, title protection).

A book title is considered like a trade mark which you automatically possess as soon as your book is published. Since it's a trade mark, you cannot have the same title as another book to avoid confusion (this is oversimplified, but I hope you forgive me for not writing this in Legalese). This also goes for similar titles that aren't word-for-word the same - the rule of thumb is that if readers could get the two titles mixed up, it's better to look for a different one.

Some authors simply use different punctuation, add a subtitle or slightly change word order - those are all in a bit of a grey zone. You could risk it, but if you end up going against a big publisher, the gamble might not pay off.

If you really, really want to use an existing title, get in touch with the publisher and ask if they're agreeable (get it in writing). I've heard from several indie authors who had no issue getting permission from trad publishers, especially if their genre was different to that of the existing book.

> Third parties shall be prohibited from using the commercial designation or a similar sign in trade, without authorisation, in a manner liable to cause confusion with the protected designation.

> — ACT ON THE PROTECTION OF TRADE MARKS AND OTHER SIGNS, SECTION 15

## DO YOUR RESEARCH

Sadly, there isn't a simple way of seeing all existing book titles in one place. I'm sorry, but you're going to have to spend some time on research. Again. As I said already, dealing with translations is all about research.

If you want to make sure your intended title hasn't been used already, do NOT rely on simply searching Amazon. Check several retailers, both online and brick-and-mortar chains like Thalia or Hugendubel. If you've not found a book with that title at retailers and Google, search buchhandel.de, a platform run by the Verzeichnis Lieferbarer Bucher (VLB, directory of available books). If you want to be extra thorough, search the German National Library at dnb.de.

As your last step, check the three magazines mentioned below.

It's your responsibility to make sure not to use a title someone else is already using. Don't assume that because you're an indie author, the other publisher will be lenient. Better safe than sorry.

---

## PROTECTING YOUR TITLE

A title generally isn't protected until you publish the book, whether it's a pre-order or a live release. If you want to 'reserve' your book title while you're still getting ready to publish, you can do so up to six months before your publication date by advertising in one of the three main book magazines. If you're planning an entire series in German, I recommend reserving all titles at the same time (as long as they all release within 6 months) to save money.

**Börsenblatt**: €50 for the first title, €5.80 for each additional title in the same ad (plus VAT)

https://www.boersenblatt.net/service/titelschutz

**BuchMarkt**: €27.50 for the ad, €2.50 for each title (plus VAT)

https://buchmarkt.de/titelschutz/

**Der Titelschutzanzeiger**: €110

https://www.titelschutzanzeiger.de

Link to form: https://www.titelschutzanzeiger.de/auftragsformular/

There are several others like Titelschutz-Magazin and Titelschutz Journal. It doesn't matter which one you use, so feel free to simply choose the cheapest one as long as it's not specific to one genre or geographical region other than Germany.

An ad will look like this:

Unter Hinweis auf §§ 5, 15 MarkenG wird Titelschutz in Anspruch genommen für:
TITLE
in jeder Schreibweise, Darstellungsform, Wortverbindung und Kombination zur Verwendung in allen Medien.
PUBLISHER
ADDRESS

*With reference to §§ 5, 15 of the Trade Mark Act, title protection is claimed for TITLE in any spelling, form of presentation, word combination and combination for use in all media.*

Do you need to do this? If your title is something very specific, it's unlikely anyone else will choose the same title and it'll be enough to take advantage of automatic (and free) title protection when you publish. If you've found a title that's quite generic but has miraculously not been used by others, it can be advisable to reserve it unless you can put up the pre-order right away.

What happens if someone ends up using your title after you've published?

Well, technically you can take them to court. Of course, this will cost both money and time, so you might want to think about contacting the other author/publisher and try to find a solution that way. You could formally agree that both of you are allowed to use the same title. One official way this can be done is by advertising both titles side by side in one of the title protection magazines.

If you don't act on someone using your title for three years, your entitlement to title protection ends.

---

*Side note: Officially copyrighting a title is something relatively new and generally only relevant if you want to extend your reach to merchandising, courses and other non-book products. If you're planning to build an Harry-Potter-style empire, get in touch with a German lawyer before deciding on a title.*

---

## RESOURCES

- Act on the Protection of Trade Marks and other Signs: https://www.gesetze-im-internet.de/englisch_markeng/englisch_markeng.html
- FAQ about Titelschutz (in German): https://www.boersenblatt.net/titelschutz/faq
- Buchhandel search: Buchandel.de
- German National Library: https://www.dnb.de/

# BLURB

While you might be tempted to simply have your existing book blurb translated, there are some key differences that you have to be aware of.

- German blurbs are generally shorter than English ones (as always, there are genre-specific differences). Keep your blurb to under 100 words. Be concise, don't give away too much.
- Don't use quotes by English magazines or by authors who don't have any German translations. Your target audience won't know them. Of course, if you have a quote by a big German author or magazine, pimp the hell out of it!
- You can use a tag line at the top of the blurb but not many German authors do.
- In English blurbs, we're used to a paragraph at the end with more information on the book, the genre, and often a 'scroll up and buy' message. You'll almost never find this in German blurbs and if you

do, it's often for indie books translated from English.

If your translator is experienced, they might be able to rewrite your English blurb into one that conforms to German standards. Alternatively, you can write a new one and have that translated.

---

## RESOURCES

- Buchdeals guide to blurbs (in German): https://autoren.buchdeals.de/blurb-richtig-schreiben/
- Blurb formatting tool: https://kindlepreneur.com/amazon-book-description-generator/

# BIO

There's not much to say about bios – they aren't very different from what we use in English. You could simply translate your existing bio into German, but I recommend adjusting it a little to cater to your new audience.

- Keep it short, write it in third person, highlight where you live (especially if it's an exotic or unusual place).
- If you mention bestseller titles or awards by name, make sure they're big enough to mean something to your German audience. If not, go with a generic 'award-winning'.
- If you write in several genres but only translate one genre, adjust your bio to focus on the themes of your German translations rather than all your existing books.

# COVERS

Covers sell books. You might already have a stunning cover for your English originals, but will it work for a German audience?

When I first started looking into translations, I didn't even think that I might have to change my covers - until I looked through German retailers and saw just how different cover trends are.

In some genres, you're lucky and cover conventions won't differ much. You might be able to keep your covers. In others, they're vastly different and it would be advisable to get new covers done by a German designer.

Since this book isn't aimed at a particular genre, I won't go into too much detail. I encourage you to do your own research specific to your genre. Look at both trad and indie covers by German authors. Avoid looking at other translations because you can't be sure they followed the German trends rather than the ones they're used to from their home market.

*(Tiny problem with that: many German authors use an English-sounding pen name, sometimes even an English title. If you're not sure where an author is from, check their bio or website.)*

I've already said it before, but don't just look at Amazon but also at other retailers.

## WHAT SHOULD BE ON THE COVER?

As mentioned in Bestseller lists, the majority of German covers don't show a bestseller title above the author name. Author names aren't always centred either, you'll often find them on the left or right of the cover.

Traditionally published books have their logo on the front cover, usually on the bottom (left, right or centred). Some indies do the same, but it's not a necessity. I always have my publisher logo on the spine and back, but so far, I've not started adding it to the front.

## PRINT COVERS

If you're planning on offering a print version of your book (highly recommended), you'll be wondering what size your wrap should be.

Sadly, there is no simple answer to this question.

I had a look at five random books in different genres:

1. Fantasy: 13.5 x 21.1 cm
2. Thriller: 12.8 x 18.8 cm
3. Contemporary romance: 12.4 x 18.8 cm
4. Non-fiction: 12.8 x 16.8 cm
5. Historical: 13 x 19 cm

Notice something? None of them are the same. I promise I didn't try and find five different ones, I simply clicked on the first book that came up for each genre. And in case you thought those were genre conventions, you're sadly wrong. Take five books within a genre and you'll once again end up with several different sizes.

To decide on a trim size, let's have a look at which ones the tools many of us use support.

Vellum offers 12 x 19 cm, 12.5 x 19 cm and 13.5 x 21.5 cm (the size of the fantasy novel) for formatting, but KDP doesn't have these as a standard size. While you can upload to KDP by entering custom dimensions, it'll make the book ineligible for extended distribution, meaning your book will only be sold on Amazon and not at other retailers. If you want extended distribution, the closest KDP standard sizes are 5 x 8 in (12.7 x 20.32 cm) and 5.06 x 7.81 in (12.85 x 19.84 cm) - both of these are available to choose from in Vellum also.

In the end, it'll be your and your designer's choice which size to go with. At least you can be sure that German readers won't mind if your book is a certain size - they're used to their book shelves not looking perfectly even. The only concrete advice I can give you is to stick to narrow widths (the widest book among those sampled was only 5.4 in).

Something else you should be aware of is that the spine text is the other way round in German. The title is usually at the top of the spine, rotated 90 degrees to the left, then beneath that the author name, then the publisher's name and/or logo. If you have a large spine, title and author name are often parallel, either rotated by 90 degrees or with no rotation.

## RESOURCES

One website promising to give you feedback on your cover is 'Cover Bewerten' (Rate a Cover) where you can upload your cover and blurb for free and hope that others will give you a rating from 1 to 5. While it's a great concept, I didn't get a single rating during the entire month I had one of my covers on the site. I'm only mentioning the site in case it gets resuscitated in the future.

- Cover Bewerten: https://www.cover-bewerten.de/
- Cover designer listings on Selfpublishing Market: https://www.selfpublishingmarkt.de/listing-category/cover-design/
- Facebook group for German covers: https://www.facebook.com/groups/buchcover
- KDP supported trim sizes: https://kdp.amazon.com/en_US/help/topic/G201834180#trim
- Vellum supported trim sizes: https://help.vellum.pub/print/trim-sizes/

**6**

# INTERVIEW WITH COVER DESIGNER RENEE ROTT

**What cover trends do you see in the German market right now?**

At the moment, abstract covers without people are trendy, showing smoke or splashes of colour, for example. Abstract shapes are very popular now. But I see that this trend is already waning again. Instead, English-style covers are becoming more and more popular - with lots of effects and highlights, but not as heavily painted as English covers.

**What do you recommend to authors who publish German translations - new covers or keep the existing ones?**

My recommendation would be not to put too much writing on a German cover and to keep any text rather short and concise. Also, the covers should not have too many focal points - a cover with five characters will probably not go down as well in Germany as a cover with a single focus (e.g. the main hero with strong exposure). Bright colours and effects are also very popular here. However, the pictures should not be overpainted and look too drawn or comic-like, because German readers still often interpret books with such covers as children's books.

There is also a trend among English books to keep book covers purist and to place only one detail on a single-coloured cover. In my experience, this type of cover hardly works at all in Germany.

I always recommend looking at the Top 100 of your genre. There you can find good impulses and tips on what types of covers work well. In the end, however, the cover should always represent the story and not just follow the trend, because this can disappear again quickly.

**How do German covers differ from English covers?**

English covers are usually painted over more and show more people and effects. German covers are a bit simpler and often only show one person or their face - in other words, a single focus. I also see more writing on English covers. The titles are longer and often include quotes or reviews from newspapers, bloggers or readers. That is very rare on German covers. As far as effects and highlights are concerned, however, the boundaries are gradually becoming blurred. In Germany, the styles of different genres also differ very clearly. While fantasy book covers like to be colourful and detailed, it is trendy in thrillers, for example, to show only the murder weapon or an important object in a big way on the cover and to emphasise it accordingly. You rarely see the protagonists on thriller covers.

· · ·

## Do German indie authors want their logo on the cover or is that only something for publishers?

Some of my clients want to have their logo on the cover, but that's rather rare. I would say the ratio is about 70 to 30.

---

### Renee Rott / Dream Design – Cover and Art

**Website**: http://www.cover-and-art.de

**Facebook**: http://www.facebook.com/traumdesigns

**Instagram**: http://www.instagram.com/cover.and.art

# SELECTED COVER DESIGNERS

Here are some cover artists who I've personally spoken to. They're all happy to be contacted in English.

### Renee Rott / Dream Design – Cover and Art

**Website**: http://www.cover-and-art.de

**Facebook**: http://www.facebook.com/traumdesigns

**Instagram**: http://www.instagram.com/cover.and.art

**What's the best way to contact you?** Email, Facebook or Instagram.

**Genres:** I particularly love fantasy and thriller/horror covers, but do all genres and am also very experienced with non-fiction.

**Pricing:** A complete package consisting of ebook and paperback covers and a promotional image costs €99. I also have a marketing package and a premium package for €119 and €169 respectively, which include extra things like designs for bookmarks, postcards or extra stock photos for more elaborate edits.

**Do you offer Premades**? Yes!

**Other services**: I design book covers as well as promotional materials such as bookmarks, postcards and more. I also offer logo design, book decoration and simple illustrations or help with formatting manuscripts for Amazon KDP.

**Can you be contacted in English?** Yes! I speak fluent English, so there is no language barrier for English-speaking clients :)

---

### Coverboutique Constanze Kramer

**Website**: www.coverboutique.de

**Facebook**: https://www.facebook.com/coverboutique.de

**Instagram**: https://www.instagram.com/coverboutique.de/

**What's the best way to contact you?** Email (info@ coverboutique.de), Facebook or Instagram.

**Genres:** Fantasy, Romance, Dark Romance

**Pricing:** Custom covers start at €150

**Do you offer Premades**? Yes, starting at €99

**Other services**: Formatting, promotional material

**Can you be contacted in English?** Yes

---

**Chris / Christian Eickmanns**

**Website**: writtengraphics.com

**What's the best way to contact you?** Form on website or info@writtengraphics.com

**Genres:** specialising on thriller and crime, but open to all genres

**Pricing:** from €199

**Do you offer Premades**? Not yet

**Other services**: promotional material like bookmarks, ad graphics,...

**Can you be contacted in English?** Yes

---

**miss uppercover** | Andrea Janas

**Website: missuppercover.com**

**Instagram**: https://www.instagram.com/missuppercover/

**What's the best way to contact you?** hello@missuppercover.com or website form

**Genres:** fiction, non-fiction, new/young adult, romance, children's books, travel, cookbooks – pretty much everything except fantasy and crime/thriller

**Pricing:** from €500

**Do you offer Premades**? yes

**Other services**: formatting, promo graphics, 3D mockups, social media graphics, logos

**Can you be contacted in English?** Yes

# FORMATTING

I f you format your book yourself or hire a formatter used to English books, you should be aware of a few things.

### 1. Quotation marks are different

"I love books," she said.
turns into
„I love books", she said.
Or »I love books«, she said. [these marks are called *Guillemets* or *Chevrons*]

In Switzerland and Liechtenstein, Guillemets are turned the other way round, « QUOTE ».

Your translator will likely choose which version to use as the adorably named 'Gänsefüßchen' (= little geese feet): the so-called German quotation marks „ " or Guillemets. In traditional publishing, Guillemets are standard as they're seen as more elegant and easier to read, while in indie publishing this rule has been somewhat loosened.

I recommend sticking to one style in all your books, even if they're done by different translators.

## 2. Hyphenation

If you use software that doesn't have a German language setting, turn off hyphenation. The rules for hyphenation are very different and if they're set automatically it will often lead to incorrectly split words.

## 3. Dashes

Just like there are several dashes in English like the en-dash and the em-dash, there is also a (slightly confusing) variety of dashes in German. Gedankenstrich, Bis-Strich, Gegenstrich, Streckenstrich,... (if you haven't figured it out yet, Strich means dash).

This is something where you'll have to trust your translator/editor. Just be sure not to change any dashes because you think it looks wrong - and don't let your formatting programme do so either.

# IMPRINT

An Impressum (imprint) is an essential part of every book, clearly showing the reader who is responsible both for the content and the production/printing. You will need one both for your book and your website, if you have one in German. Technically, you even need one on Facebook, if you have a page specifically aimed at German readers.

But is this really necessary when you're not German and don't live in Germany?

In 2013, a German regional court decided that an Impressum is needed for international website owners if their services/advertising is directed at German consumers. As a result of this ruling, an Egyptian cruise ship company whose entire website was aimed at German customers was fined for not having a complete, proper Impressum.

While it's unlikely that anyone will report you, if you're prosecuted for violating the Impressum requirement you could be subjected to a fine of up to €5,000.

Germany is split into 16 federal states (Bundesländer) and each of them has their own regional laws. For authors living in Germany, this means they have to abide by their state's laws. For those of us who live abroad, it's a little more tricky.

The general rule across all 16 media laws is that you're required to include:

- Your name (legal name) or your company's name
- Your or your company's address
- Your printer's name and address (for books)

This throws up all sorts of problems. Many of us use pen names and don't want our legal names publicly available. The same goes for our private addresses. PO boxes don't count as as an address, you will have to provide a street address.

## BOOKS

As an author, you are legally obliged to include an Impressum in your book. This applies equally to print books and e-books. It does not matter whether the Impressum is placed at the beginning or at the end of the book. With printed books, it is usual to place the Impressum on the first pages before the actual book text begins. For eBooks, you can either put it at the beginning or the very end. The latter has the advantage that it won't be visible in the 'look inside' feature of some retailers.

If you publish through BoD or Tredition and use one of their ISBNs, they count as the publisher and you won't have to add an address.

While some authors don't credit their translators, German law requires the publisher to offer full recognition of the translator's work (since they're seen as the author of the translation). Most contracts will include a clause telling you to credit the translator.

> The author has the right to be identified as the author of the work. He may determine whether the work shall bear a designation of authorship and which designation is to be used.

> — ACT ON COPYRIGHT AND RELATED RIGHTS, SECTION 13

## WEBSITE

The requirement to have an Impressum on your website is regulated by the telemedia act (Telemediengesetz). If your website is aimed at the German market, you need to include:

- Name.
- Address.
- Email address.
- Legal form in case of a legal person and its authorised representative and, to the extent that details are provided of the equity of the company, the share and nominal capital.
- Company registration number (if applicable)
- VAT number (if applicable)

This information has to be easily accessible for users. It's best to make a page just for the Impressum and link to it from the main menu or the footer of your website. You also need to have a privacy policy to inform your users about the collection, processing and use of personal data. This must include a description on the use of cookies, if applicable.

## POTENTIAL WAYS AROUND THIS

- Rent a virtual address (not a PO box)
- If you have an agent, ask if you can use their address
- Some authors use pseudonym or imprint services, but as you read in the Interview with Arno Lampmann, those can't be used for this.

---

## RESOURCES

- tolino blog about imprints (in German): https://blog.tolino-media.de/2020/06/impressum-was-ist-pflicht-was-ist-kuer/
- Thomson Reuters Practical Law: Digital business in Germany: https://uk.practicallaw.thomsonreuters.com/5-637-9385

# IMPRESSUM TEMPLATE

Here's a template for an Impressum that you're free to use.

IMPRESSUM

*Book title*
Autor: *Author name*
Übersetzung: *Translator name*
Umschlaggestaltung: *Cover designer name*
Satz: *Formatter name*
Verlag: *Publisher name (if applicable)*

Die Originalausgabe erschien *year of original* unter dem Titel "*original title*".

© *YEAR Name of Author/Copyright holder.*

Alle Rechte vorbehalten.

Autor: *First name, last name*
*Contact details (address, email address)*

ISBN: xxx-x-xxxxx-xxx-x

Druck: *printing company*

---

*[if applicable]*

Bibliografische Information der Deutschen Nationalbibliothek:

Die Deutsche Nationalbibliothek verzeichnet diese Publikation in der Deutschen Nationalbibliografie; detaillierte bibliografische Daten sind im Internet über http://dnb.d- nb.de abrufbar.

# 11

# METADATA: CATEGORIES

While each retailer uses their own way of categorising books, most of their classification systems are based on one of the numerous subject or book classification schemes used around the world.

It can be confusing once you realise just how many systems there are. BISAC, BIC, Thema, WGSneu, CLIL,... And of course, not all distributors/retailers use the same. That would be way too easy.

I recommend making a list with the categories you'll be using again in the future, that way it'll become much easier for your next books.

## BISAC

BISAC categories are used by most North America based retailers and distributors including Draft2Digital and Publishdrive. Amazon's categories are based on BISAC with a few variations.

Some German retailers/distributors use BISAC as well, sometimes in combination with other systems like Thema.

**Subject headings list**: https://bisg.org/page/bisacedition

## THEMA

Thema is a multilingual category scheme used worldwide that's based on BIC (which is now slowly being retired). Thema is relatively new, launched at the Frankfurt Book Fair in 2012. They use letters for their classification, adding more and more letters the further you dive into a category.

 **Example**

> F: Fiction and related items
>
> FR: Romance
>
> FRT: Romance: fantasy and paranormal

In addition to the subject catgories, Thema also has qualifiers to describe a book even further. These include geographic qualifiers, age groups, languages, and many others.

If our example paranormal romance is for young adults and is set in the Scottish Orkney islands in 2008, we can add the following:

3MRBA: 2000 to 2009

5AT: age 16+

1DDU-GB-SHF: Orkney Islands

This makes it extremely specific and helps retailers and librarians who're looking for a very particular book.

What I like about Thema is that they have usage notes for their categories which can help you decide if that category is suitable for your book.

### ❝ Example for Romance: fantasy and paranormal (FRT)

*Class here: vampire romance, were / shifter romance. Use for: a romance story which blends elements from the fantasy genre or features mythical creatures or supernatural elements but remain primarily and recognisably a romance story.*

Ingram Spark and Feiyr are some of the distributors using Thema, while Apple is one of the retailers who support the scheme.

**Category list:** https://ns.editeur.org/thema/en

**In German:** https://ns.editeur.org/thema/de

## WGSNEU

The new Warengruppen-Systematik (WGSneu) is a revamp of a classification scheme that has been used in the German book market since 1997.

It's quite sparse in terms of fiction categories and you'll get frustrated quickly if you're trying to find a romance category - there isn't one. Romance authors will either have to use a genre like historical fiction or fantasy fiction, or go with something generic such as contemporary fiction (Gegenwartsliteratur).

Google Play uses this system for German books.

. . .

List of WGSneu categories (pdf, in German): https://vlb.de/
assets/images/wgsneuversion2_o.pdf

# 12

# ISBN

To ISBN or not to ISBN, that's the question. It's a discussion that pops up again and again, not just in relation to translations, but among all self-publishers. Every book has an ISBN, the issue is whether you decide to get your own or not.

ISBN stands for **International Standard Book Number.** Its purpose is to uniquely identify a title or edition of a title from one specific publisher. An ISBN is good for only one format of your book, so you'd need two ISBNs for an eBook and a paperback version. Think of it as a fingerprint: everyone's fingerprint is unique, even that of identical twins whose content is the same. Okay, scratch that metaphor. Basically, every version of your book needs a new ISBN, which includes translations.

Most indie authors don't use an ISBN for their eBook, choosing instead to use free ISBNs or identifiers offered by retailers. However, this results in the retailer or distributor being recorded as the publisher rather than yourself, and is the reason why organisations like the Alliance of

Independent Authors (ALLI) recommend you get your own ISBNs.

For paperbacks, it's a different matter. If you're only going to sell your paperbacks via Amazon and its expanded distribution, you don't necessarily need one. If, however, you want your books to be sold in shops and libraries, you'll need to use a distributor like Ingram Spark (more on that later) who require you to buy your own ISBN.

You will have to purchase your ISBN from your country's agency (in the US it would be Bowker, here in the UK it's Nielsen). It goes by country of residence, not nationality. Many agencies offer a whole set of ISBNs for less than if you were to buy them individually, so if you're going to publish several books, buy in bulk.

In some countries like Canada, ISBNs are issued for free. Lucky Canucks.

All of this is also valid for translations. It's your own decision whether to use an ISBN for the eBook. Depending on how you distribute your print version, you may or may not have to buy one. ISBNs become important if you want to be listed in the Verzeichnis Lieferbarer Bücher (VLB), the catalogue that German booksellers use to find books to purchase. We'll discuss this in Getting into book shops and libraries.

In case you were wondering, you can't buy a German ISBN unless you live in Germany.

## RESOURCES

- ALLI Guide to ISBNs: https://
  selfpublishingadvice.org/isbns-for-authors/
- Find your country's ISBN agency: https://www.
  isbn-international.org/agencies
- 'What is an ISBN' on Kindlepreneur: https://
  kindlepreneur.com/what-is-isbn/

# 13

## PRICING

As mentioned in the introduction, German prices are written with the currency symbol after the price and instead of a full stop, a comma is used before decimals, e.g. 2,99€. Germany and Austria both use the Euro (€ or EUR) as their currency while Switzerland and Liechtenstein use the Swiss franc (CHF).

VAT on books is a reduced rate of 7% and is included in prices shown to consumers.

All retailers allow you to adjust individual countries' prices. Be sure to make the price 'pretty' by having it end in .99 (or .49 if you really must). Anything else looks unprofessional and might even result in less sales.

Research into psychological pricing tells us that buyers prefer prices that end in .99. One study conducted by the University of Chicago and the MIT gave a group of women the choice of buying an item of clothing at either $34, $39 or $44. Even though $34 was the cheapest, most sales happened at $39. Nine is the magic number, so use it!

## BUCHPREISBINDUNG

Since 2002, German law requires a book to be sold at a fixed price everywhere. Since 2016, this also applies to eBooks. This means retailers can't run sales and promotions. For you as an author, this is actually beneficial: you always get the same royalty and you can be assured that when you tell readers your book is available for €9,99, it won't be cheaper or more expensive at their local book store.

There are exceptions for used books as well as lower preorder prices.

It's your responsibility to ensure that your book is sold at the same price everywhere. If you put a book on sale, it has to be on sale *everywhere*. By the way, all the main retailers require you to do this in their terms of service, so you should be having the same price everywhere anyway.

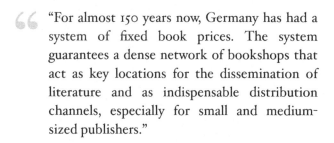 "For almost 150 years now, Germany has had a system of fixed book prices. The system guarantees a dense network of bookshops that act as key locations for the dissemination of literature and as indispensable distribution channels, especially for small and medium-sized publishers."

— ALEXANDER SKIPIS, MANAGING
DIRECTOR OF THE BÖRSENVEREIN

## EBOOKS

In Germany, eBooks are generally more expensive than what you might be used to. This is mostly due to the fact that trad publishing still dominates the market. In 2020, the average price for an eBook was €6.63, slightly more than the year before, although that's a deep drop from €10.70 in 2010. A recent study, the 'digital consumer book barometer', found two sweet spots for eBooks in the German-speaking market: €4-5 and €8-9.

I generally recommend adding at least one Euro to your English price. Of course, pricing depends a lot on genre, just like it does in English-speaking markets, so take a look at what similar authors are doing.

> "Don't bother with 99c. Price German books at 3.99 or higher as readers are prepared to pay a higher price."

> — MILA YOUNG

Having a permafree first-in-series is a strategy that can work in Germany just like it does in the English-speaking market. I personally waited until my first series was complete before I started experimenting with permafrees.

## PRINT BOOKS

On average, a paperback costs just under €11 in Germany. If you include all formats including hardcovers, that average jumps to around €14.

More than two thirds of books are priced at over €10.

A look at the current SPIEGEL Bestseller list (July 2021) shows that the cheapest paperback costs €10 while the cheapest hardcover is priced at €14 (although that's an outlier, most start at around €20).

Indie books are generally cheaper. I had a look at 20 bestselling indie paperbacks on Thalia and found that most prices lie between €8.90 and €14.90. Very few indie authors have hardcovers, but when they do, they're usually priced a few Euros more than the paperback edition.

## RESOURCES

- Free Reedsy course on international book pricing: https://blog.reedsy.com/learning/courses/distribution/pricing-books-international/
- The digital consumer book barometer 2021: https://www.dropbox.com/s/ey4shka0f2rpcbk/2021_Digital-Consumer-Book-Barometer_final.pdf

# 14

# PAYING AND GETTING PAID

W e've talked a lot about both spending and earning money in this book, so let's look at that in more detail. Dealing with translations means lots of international money transfers, both from and to you. Of course, you could use your normal bank account in your country, but that will results in fees and possibly not the best exchange rates.

While you may be used to using Paypal to pay designers, editors and so on, I don't recommend them for international payments as their fees are very high and their currency exchange rate is worse than in other places. While you can send free 'friends and family' transactions within your own country, it isn't free for transfers between other countries.

Instead of Paypal I like to use Wise (formerly Transferwise), which not only has much lower fees but also gives you the option to open virtual bank accounts in several countries including the EU.

I get my Amazon EU royalties paid to my EU Wise account, which I then use to pay for author services, plus I can wait for the exchange rate to be at an optimal level before converting the EUR to GBP. Their Mastercard also comes in very handy when visiting Germany to pay in shops and restaurants with no currency conversion fees.

Both Amazon and Google allow you to set up several bank accounts that you can assign individual currencies to. If you think of this as a lot of unnecessary work, let me tell you a story. I live in the UK and when I first started publishing, I set up Amazon to pay into my UK bank account. One month, I realised that I'd received almost £200 less than I'd expected from looking at sales reports. Had Amazon made a mistake? No. Turns out the USD to GBP exchange rate had changed dramatically between the month I'd sold the books and the month I was actually paid. Even though technically, I'd been sent the correct amount, I still felt cheated. Ever since, I have several bank accounts set up on both Amazon and Google: my normal UK one, a Wise account for USD and since I started translations a Wise account for Euros. I have alerts set up that tell me when the exchange rate is favourable and that's when I convert my other currencies to GBP and transfer the money to my normal bank account.

Of course, Wise isn't the only option, it's just my favourite one after trying several other tools.

. . .

If you only want to send money, CurrencyFair is another good alternative that I have used myself in the past. They have a recurring payment option which could be used for payment plans if your translator offers those.

A third option is Payoneer, which like Wise provides you with a Mastercard and a local EU bank account, although with that you can only receive, not send money. You can only send money to other Payoneer users, which is a bit restricting.

Most German retailers and distributors will pay you via bank transfer. Some offer Paypal. Cheques haven't been used in Germany for several decades and most people wouldn't know what to do with them.

---

**Resources**

- Wise: https://transferwise.com/ (referral link which gives you a free international transfer)
- CurrencyFair: https://www.currencyfair.com/de/rafland/?channel=RE5OH1 (referral link)
- Payoneer: https://www.payoneer.com/

# PUBLISHING CHOICES

# 1

## KINDLE UNLIMITED VS WIDE

N ow that you've got your finished translation, it's time to publish.

First of all, just like with your English originals, you will have to decide whether to go into Kindle Unlimited and be exclusive to Amazon, or whether you'll go wide and reach a lot more retailers.

I could write an entire book about Kindle Unlimited (KU) vs Wide (= being on all retailers and not exclusive to Amazon), but you can find that discussion in many other places. I can highly recommend the book Wide for the Win by Mark Leslie Lefebvre and the Facebook group by the same name, if you want more on why and how to be wide.

You may be tempted to take the same route as you did for your English books, but there are some differences in the German market that you should be aware of.

. . .

**Pros**:

- KU can help attract readers who might otherwise not pick up a new author (remember, you're back to being a new author).
- Better ranks will give you more visibility.
- Lucrative All-Star Bonuses are easier to get on Amazon.de than in the UK and US. Instead of 100 authors, the top 150 authors will get a bonus payment ranging from €500 to €7,500 (although that's quite low compared to Amazon US's $25k). There's another bonus for the top 100 titles that will add between €250 and €750 to your monthly income. There is no bonus for illustrated books like there is for the UK and US.
- Your book is eligible for participation in Prime Reading.

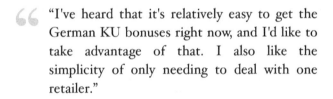

"I've heard that it's relatively easy to get the German KU bonuses right now, and I'd like to take advantage of that. I also like the simplicity of only needing to deal with one retailer."

— EVA CHASE

**Cons**:

- KU is available in Germany, but not in Austria and Switzerland. You're therefore missing out on a chunk of the German-speaking readership.
- As discussed in Statistics, over 40 per cent of the German eBook market is taken up by the tolino alliance of retailers. Even if the other retailers are

only 10 per cent of the market, that still means Amazon only has half the market. That's a big chunk to miss out on.

- You only get 5 free days a term in KU while if you're wide, you can choose when and for how long you want to make your book free.

> "I like wide because I hate getting ripped off, which is what I feel when I'm in KU, and I don't like monopolies or having all my eggs in one basket."
>
> — DIONNE LISTER

Personally, I decided to go wide with my translations, just like I'm wide with all my English books. I know of other authors who put their first German translation into KU for a term to gather reviews and potentially a bestseller title, then took it wide. There are pros and cons about that too, but again, there are many other books dealing with the KU/wide issue.

Looking at the results of my survey, two fifths put their books into Kindle Unlimited, one quarter went wide and the rest tried both, depending on the book.

---

## RESOURCES

- 'Wide for the Win' by Mark Leslie Lefebvre: https://books2read.com/wideforthewin
- Wide for the Win Facebook group: https://www.facebook.com/groups/wideforthewin

## 2

# SHOULD I GO DIRECT?

If you've decided to be wide, the next question is whether you'll use a distributor or go direct with retailers.

I'm an advocate of going direct with retailers whenever you can, as this will often give you more promotional opportunities plus you won't lose a share of your royalties.

However, if you're short on time and don't want to make the learning curve even steeper, it can be easier to go with a distributor.

Of course, there's no either-or. You can go direct with some retailers and use a distributor (or several) for everything else. Just be aware that some distributors require you to be exclusive with them, so this is only possible with some of them.

There are a surprising amount of distributors serving the German-language market and I'll highlight the main ones shortly, but first, let's talk about the individual retailers (starting with Amazon for everyone who's planning to be in Kindle Unlimited).

*You'll notice that I didn't include Barnes & Noble in the following chapters about retailers. They're US-based and don't sell in Europe, so while of course you can upload your books direct with them, you likely won't sell many copies and it's your choice to decide whether it's worth it.*

# RETAILERS

# AMAZON

D o I need to tell you who/what Amazon is? If so, then you're reading the wrong book. At least that makes this chapter very short and quick.

While Germany has Amazon.de, Austrian and Swiss customers don't have their own local Amazon sites and have to use the German one. Austrians get the same free Prime delivery benefits as Germans, but the Swiss have to pay for delivery and customs, which is why Amazon is only their third most popular online retailer.

Kindle Unlimited is available on Amazon.de for everyone using their site, so it's open to not just Germans, but also Austrians, Swiss, etc.

## FINDING CATEGORIES

Amazon categories vary across marketplaces and the ones you find on Amazon.de won't be the same you're used to from the US site. If you don't speak German, you'll be glad to know that you can browse Amazon.de in English, just change the language settings in the top bar if it doesn't show in English automatically.

The process of finding the perfect categories for your book isn't any different from doing it for your English books, except that you're searching Amazon.de.

You can use these shortcuts to see all categories available on Amazon.de:

- **Kindle categories:** https://www.amazon.de/s?
  bbn=530485031&rh=n%3A530484031%2Cn%
  3A530886031&dc&qid=1603391008&rnid=
  530485031&ref=sr_nr_n_2
- **Print book categories:** https://www.amazon.de/
  b%C3%BCcher-buch-lesen/b/?ie=UTF8&node=
  186606&ref_=topnav_storetab_b

You can also check similar (German) books by other authors to see what categories they're in and if they would be suitable for your book.

Once you've found the perfect categories, add two of them in KDP and email them via the dashboard help section to add eight more (you can have ten in total). Annoyingly, not all the categories you can choose when uploading a book actually exist on Amazon.de, so you'll have to double check. Only choose categories that exist on Amazon.de in that section.

Some categories you can only access by contacting KDP. Be sure to specify that you want the categories set for Amazon.de, although of course you can request categories for other marketplaces as well (and you probably should).

If you want to simplify the process, Kindlerepreneur's Publisher Rocket is a tool to find both categories and keywords on Amazon.de.

> "I used Publisher Rocket to set up my keywords the same way I do for my English titles, putting together keyword phrases that are popular. For advertising, I identified some comp authors and ran it through the AMS keyword search, then used those to get the ball rolling. I find that the automatic targeting on Amazon needs a little nudge and once it starts pairing my books to comp authors and their keywords, AMS picks up on more automatic suggestions."
>
> — TAMSIN LEY

## KEYWORDS

In this case, a translation programme might finally be the answer, hurray! Yes, you can simply drop your existing keywords into Google Translate and use the German results for your book. Of course it's more accurate to ask your translator - but I'm glad to finally give you an opportunity to use AI translation.

## A NOTE ON PRICE PROMOTIONS

If you're in KDP Select, you'll be used to Countdown Deals for short-term price drops. These are only available for the US and UK though, so if you want to do a price promo on Amazon.de, you'll have to manually lower your price.

SKYE B. MACKINNON

If you want to make your KU book free, their Free Book Promotion is worldwide.

If you're not in KDP Select and want to make your book free, you'll have to set your book to free at all other retailers and then contact KDP to price match. Specifically mention that you want it price-matched in ALL marketplaces.

---

## RESOURCES

- Publisher Rocket (affiliate link): https://publisherrocket.com/?ref=spgerman&affiliate=perytonpress
- Kindlepreneur: Finding and selecting international categories: https://kindlepreneur.com/selling-kindle-books-internationally/

**2**

# SETTING UP AUTHOR CENTRAL

Did you know you can have a German bio show on Amazon? You can add it via Author Central, which also has some other nifty functions.

## SET UP YOUR GERMAN BIO

Amazon's Author Central used to have separate sites for different countries, but they recently simplified it to have everything under one roof.

1. Go to author.amazon.com/profile.
2. Under 'Your biographies', click the 'add bio in new language' button.
3. Select German and paste in your bio.

And that's it. From now on, anyone browsing Amazon in German - no matter whether it's Amazon.de or Amazon.com - will see your German bio on your book pages and author page.

In the right sidebar, there's also a drop-down menu that lets you check how your author page will look for readers in different countries.

## ADD YOUR GERMAN BOOKS

You'll likely be used to that anyway, but just a reminder to add your German books to Author Central if they aren't populated automatically. In the top bar, go to 'Books', scroll to the bottom and click 'add book'.

The Books page also allows you to sort your books by popularity. Simply choose Amazon.de as the marketplace to get a quick idea of which of your books sell best.

## CHECK YOUR REVIEWS

You can see all your Amazon.de reviews in one place by going to 'Reports + Marketing' and then choosing Amazon.de from the marketplace drop-down menu.

You can also look at your Amazon.de sales ranks via the 'Reports + Marketing' menu.

---

## RESOURCES

author.amazon.com

# 3

## TOLINO

Tolino (yes, like several other German brands they use lower case for their brand) isn't a retailer, it's an alliance of leading German booksellers Thalia, Weltbild, Hugendubel, Mayersche Buchhandlung, Osiander and Libri plus around 1,500 affiliated, independent bookshops throughout Germany - meaning that tolino is represented in over 2,000 bookshops. Since entering the market in March 2013, the tolino alliance has successfully established itself as one of the leading brands for digital reading in German-speaking countries. They've offered the possibility of self-publishing with them directly since 2015.

In 2017, tolino was acquired by Rakuten and now uses Kobo's technology, which explains why their tolino e-readers are exact copies of Kobo e-readers, albeit with different names.

They supply online shops in Germany, Austria and Switzerland, as well as the online library Skoobe and the public library system Onleihe - we'll talk more about those in Libraries and Subscriptions.

. . .

Some of the retailers your books will be available at:

- buchhandlung.de
- buecher.de
- ebook.de
- hugendubel.de
- libris.nl
- mayersche.de
- osiander.de
- paagman.nl
- standaardboekhandel.be
- thalia.de, thalia.at & orellfuessli.ch
- weltbild.de, weltbild.at & weltbild.ch
- Skoobe (optional)
- Onleihe.net (optional)
- Public libraries (optional)

As of spring 2021, you can also use tolino as a one-stop distributor who sends your books to Amazon, Google Play, Kobo, Barnes & Noble, Apple Books, Libreka, Ceebo, Ciando, Beam, mojoreads and their partners.

While you can choose whether you want to include Amazon, you can't pick and choose between the others, so you have to use tolino for all these retailers if you decide to take this route.

If you only want to be direct with Amazon, this new distribution option would be a good way to reach all the important retailers in one go.

tolino also offer to send your mandatory deposit copy to the German National Library free of charge.

To go direct with tolino, you don't have to live in Germany or Europe, but you do need an IBAN number for payments. If your bank account doesn't have one, then you may want to consider opening an account with an online bank like Wise (which has lots of advantages that I'll talk about in How to get paid).

The alternative is going through a distributor such as Draft2Digital, but this means you won't be eligible for their in-house promotions.

Their website is in German (easy to navigate in Chrome with Google Translate turned on), but their team speaks excellent English and is always happy to help. Uploading a book is easy, but be aware that you need your final files even if you want to set up a pre-order. You can format your blurb using HTML to use formatting like bold text or italics.

Officially, it can take up to 48 hours for your book to pass quality control, but it's usually only been a few hours for me.

I recently updated the backmatter for all my German books and tolino was the easiest and fastest to upload all the files to, hands down.

One issue I regularly have is having to revise my page count. In their metadata section, they ask for the page count, so I always enter the print page count - but that's often higher than their e-reader page count (which of course I don't know). They'll tell you the correct number and you then have to change it. Not a big issue, but keep an eye on your emails after submitting your book just in case.

· · ·

tolino offers a range of marketing opportunities, more on that later, but you only have access to them if you're direct, so I wholeheartedly recommend signing up for an account.

Here are some helpful hints from their marketing team:

 "I recommend that all authors contact the distributor of their choice early on, who can then give very specific tips, depending on the book, series, etc.

It is also helpful to look at similar titles from the competition. What prices do they use? What do their covers look like? The covers in particular can differ considerably from country to country - tastes are different.

When translating titles into another language, make sure that puns, idioms and common expressions are adapted accordingly, otherwise it may seem bumpy or even mean something different. We are all familiar with these "false friends".

Also be careful with German umlauts [ä, ö, ü]! If you are writing with a keyboard that does not support umlauts, make sure you use the correct special characters. Otherwise it can happen that an "Ä" or a letter with an accent looks correct in your author account, but is displayed in the shops with two characters. This not only looks unattractive, but also means that the eBook cannot be found via the search function when entering the title."

— MARTINA RASCHKE, TOLINO

You can also find a lot of helpful tips on their blog (in German).

If you have a website in German, tolino offers free 'bookview' widgets. As an added bonus, you can add affiliate codes (AWIN and Tradedoubler).

## IN SUMMARY

**Royalty rate**: 70% for €2.99 or over, 40% for under €2.99 (minus 5% tax)
**Fees**: none
**Formats accepted**: epub, doc
**Pre-orders**: final file needed
**Payment**: monthly via bank transfer (IBAN needed), minimum €20. A payment summary will be available around two weeks after the end of the month, payment will arrive in your bank account within 40 days of that.
**Exclusivity**: none
**ISBN**: free
**DRM**: no
**Devices**: tolino e-reader, mobile app, webreader in browser

## RESOURCES

- Website (in German): https://www.tolino-media.de/
- Blog (in German): https://blog.tolino-media.de
- Bookview widgets: https://affiliate.mytolino.com/index.html
- HTML blurb formatting tool: https://

kindlepreneur.com/amazon-book-description-generator/

- Information about reaching Skoobe via tolino (in German): https://blog.tolino-media.de/2020/08/skoobe-euer-weg-in-die-digitale-bibliothek/

# 4

# APPLE BOOKS

Apple Books (formerly iBooks) sells both eBooks and audiobooks to anyone owning an Apple device. Because the app comes pre-installed on all iOS phones, tablets and Mac computers, you can potentially reach over a billion people in 51 countries. In Germany, about a third of mobile phones are iPhones.

You can go direct with Apple, uploading via iTunes Connect (on Mac) or the fairly new Apple Books for Authors portal (browser based), or use pretty much any distributor. Audiobooks can only be uploaded via a distributor.

One feature that you can take advantage of when you upload direct is adding a custom sample to your book (including a preorder) to control exactly what your potential readers see.

Apple have merchandisers who curate the German-language Apple Books store. Your best chance for your book to be shown are high sales, but you can also tip the scales in your favour by linking to Apple from your websites and tagging Apple Books in social media posts. I once got a promotion for a preorder (in English) after tagging Apple on Twitter.

You can find out more about Apple promotions in the retailer promotions chapter.

## IN SUMMARY

**Royalty rate**: 70%
**Fees**: none
**Formats accepted**: epub
**Payment**: bank transfer
**Exclusivity**: no
**ISBN**: free
**DRM**: author's decision
**Devices**: no ereaders but available on all Apple devices
**Website:** https://books.apple.com/book-store

---

## RESOURCES

- Apple Books for Authors: https://authors. apple.com/
- Apple marketing services: https://tools. applemediaservices.com/

**5**

# KOBO

I'm mostly mentioning Kobo because they're usually one of the top retailers when you're wide. They offer eBooks to customers in 190 countries - it doesn't get much more international than that.

They have a German store (https://www.kobo.com/de/de) but it's not one of their priorities because of one simple reason: they've partnered with tolino.

tolino's e-readers are basically Kobo clones. For example, the Kobo Libra H2O (my favourite ever e-Reader) has been renamed to Vision 5, but is essentially the same. Instead of the Kobo store, the tolino devices access books in the tolino ecosystem. But because of their partnership, any books you upload to Kobo will also be available

Kobo has a subscription programme called Kobo Plus which is currently available in Belgium, the Netherlands and Canada. With almost three quarters of Dutch speaking German, enrolling in the programme could be well worth it. You can also use Kobo to upload to Overdrive to reach over 20,000 libraries worldwide.

Kobo offers great promotions for English-language books, but currently doesn't offer any for German books. For more, see the Retailer promotion chapter.

Kobo is the only retailer that doesn't let you enter a translator in the metadata. As an alternative, you could add them as an author or mention them in the blurb.

If you don't want to go direct with Kobo, you can reach them via pretty much every distributor.

## IN SUMMARY

**Royalty rate**: 70% (45% for under €1.99)
**Fees**: none
**Formats accepted**: doc, epub
**Payment**: bank transfer
**Exclusivity**: no
**ISBN**: free
**DRM**: author's choice
**Devices**: Kobo e-readers e.g. Kobo Libra H2O
**Website**: https://www.kobo.com/de/de
**Language**: English, German & many others

---

## RESOURCES

- More about Kobo Plus: https://kobowritinglife.zendesk.com/hc/en-us/articles/360058975432-What-is-Kobo-Plus-

- Kobo help pages with guide for new authors:
  https://kobowritinglife.zendesk.com/

## 6

# GOOGLE BOOKS

Google Books, Google's very own eBook and audiobook platform, is available in 75 different countries reaching over 3 billion users. Almost two thirds of mobile phones in Germany run on Android, giving you a massive potential audience since they all come with the Google Books app pre-installed.

You can go direct with Google Books via their Google Play Books Partner Center or you can go via a distributor (although many of them require you to have an account with the Partner Center).

When uploading a book, Google lets you choose from several categorisation schemes, including one specific to the German market. Read the Metadata: Categories chapter for more on different category systems.

At the bottom of the 'book info' page, you can add 'related books'. There's an option for 'is other-language version of', so if your English books are wide as well, you can link them through that. I can't tell you if this makes any difference, but Google's algorithms are vast and complicated, so who knows, it might help.

Google Play offers you to enter pricing for almost every currency you can imagine. You can spend as much or as little time on this as you want, although I recommend you definitely enter at the very least prices for EUR, CHF and USD. For CHF and EUR, click the 'tax included' buttons.

Note that Google Play requires you to upload files for pre-orders. I know of some authors who upload placeholders, but I've heard from Google Play reps that they frown upon that practice.

Google offers a book preview widget that you can embed in your website which will take readers straight to the Google Play store if they like the sample.

## IN SUMMARY

**Royalty rate**: 70%
**Fees**: no
**Formats accepted**: epub
**Payment**: bank transfer
**Exclusivity**: no
**ISBN**: free
**DRM**: author's decision
**Devices**: Android phones & tablets
**Website**: https://play.google.com/store/books

## RESOURCES

- Publish on Google Play: https://play.google.com/books/publish/
- Preview wizard: https://developers.google.com/books/docs/preview-wizard

# DISTRIBUTORS

# 7

# SHOULD I USE A DISTRIBUTOR?

The question whether to go direct or use a distributor is one you'll likely have asked yourself already when you published your books in English. Still, there are a few differences.

**Why publish via a distributor?**

The biggest advantage is saving time and effort. By using a distributor (also known as aggregator), you don't have to deal with any administrative and technical problems of the individual shops. This is especially helpful if you don't speak any German and don't want to fuss around with translating retailers' websites. You also get into some distribution channels you couldn't reach directly - including libraries. All your royalties will come from one source as well, making finances a lot easier, especially when you consider currency conversions.

. . .

**What are the disadvantages?**

You miss out on money. Sometimes, a lot of money. Every distributor takes a cut (except for PublishDrive who have a monthly fee instead), but the amount varies. You also won't have access to some in-house promotions, e.g. at Tolino. Plus you give up a certain amount of control and sometimes enter into an exclusive contract, which limits your own flexibility.

In this chapter, we're taking a closer look at 13 different distributors. Four of them are mainly catering to English-speaking authors (Draft2Digital, PublishDrive, Streetlib and Smashwords), while the rest are focusing on the German market.

At the end of the chapter, we'll look at different ways of combining the distributors if you want to have the highest chance of reaching every single retailer, no matter how small.

I've added a little summary at the end of every retailer's section.

**Distributes to**
**Can you exclude retailers?**
**Royalty rate**
**Fees**
**Payment**
**Exclusivity**
**ISBN**
**Print-on-demand**
**Audiobooks**
**Website**

**Language**

If you've decided to be exclusive with Amazon, you can skip this section and move on to the print books section.

---

## RESOURCES

- Comparison of 11 retailers and distributors (in German): https://indie-autoren-buecher.de/ selfpublishing-blog/buch-veroeffentlichen-als- selfpublisher-anbietervergleich/
- Spreadsheet by Indie Autor with details about all the main distributors (from 2016): https://docs. google.com/spreadsheets/u/0/d/ 1woe5EKJ9E1PLcWqDPBTITsAVYcH_E2hl8yIO pmY91ZI/pub?single=true&gid=0&output=html

## 8

# DRAFT2DIGITAL

Founded in 2012, Draft2Digital is one of the best-known aggregators in the indie world. They offer eBook and print (currently in beta) distribution to all the main retailers, libraries and - most importantly for our case - the tolino network.

From personal experience I can say that they're a joy to work with and are always keen to help authors in any way they can. They offer regular promotional opportunities at retailers and libraries, although so far, there have been none for German.

Draft2Digital has a free automatic formatting feature (which can be used even if you don't use them to distribute your books) that's a good alternative to paid software such as Vellum.

They also have a new payment splitting feature that could be used to pay your translator if you have a royalty share agreement.

And finally, they run the Books2read universal link platform which I will talk more about in Sell your book.

---

**Distributes to:** all the main retailers incl tolino network, libraries, smaller stores
**Can you exclude retailers?** yes
**Royalty rate**: 85% of net royalties
**Fees**: none
**Payment**: PayPal, cheque, direct deposit, Payoneer
**Exclusivity**: no
**ISBN**: free
**Own store:** no
**Print-on-demand**: yes (beta)
**Audiobooks**: via Findaway Voices
**Website**: https://www.draft2digital.com/
**Language**: English
**Blog**: https://www.draft2digital.com/blog/

## 9

# PUBLISHDRIVE

PublishDrive is unique in that they don't take a cut of royalties but instead charge a monthly fee. It starts at $9.99 for two books and goes up to $99.99 for up to 48 books (if you have more, you'll have to contact them for pricing). It's slightly cheaper if you pay annually instead of monthly.

On one hand, that's an advantage if you use them to distribute to all or many of the big retailers and get a decent income. On the other hand, if you only want to use them for the small retailers and libraries you can't go direct with or can't reach through other distributors, you'll have to calculate if the monthly fee is worth it.

They told me they currently don't have any promotional opportunities for the German market, but that could change in future.

**Distributes to:** all the main retailers incl tolino network, libraries, smaller stores

**Can you exclude retailers?** yes

**Royalty rate**: 100% of net royalties

**Fees**: $9.99 - $99.99/month depending on number of books

**Payment**: wire transfer (via Wise), local bank transfer, check, PayPal, Payoneer or intercash

**Exclusivity**: no

**ISBN**: free

**Own store:** no

**Print-on-demand**: yes (Amazon only)

**Audiobooks**: yes

**Website**: https://publishdrive.com

**Blog**: https://publishdrive.com/blog.html

**Language**: English

# STREETLIB

Streetlib is an Italian-based distributor delivering to 76 partners. They call themselves "the widest worldwide distribution network". Just like Draft2Digital and PublishDrive, they distribute to tolino, letting you get your eBooks into all the major German book stores.

At the time of writing, they only provide print-on-demand in Italy, but they're planning to expand this in the future.

---

**Distributes to:** all the main retailers incl tolino, libraries, smaller stores
**Can you exclude retailers?** yes
**Royalty rate**: 90% of net royalties
**Fees**: no (€49 for print books)
**Payment**: Paypal, Payoneer, SureRemit, bank transfer (US only)
**Exclusivity**: no
**ISBN**: free

**Own store:** no
**Print-on-demand**: Italy only
**Audiobooks**: yes (80% net royalties)
**Website**: https://www.streetlib.com/
**Language**: English

## BOOKS ON DEMAND

B ooks on Demand (Bod) was one of the first print-on-demand platforms and distributors for self-publishers, founded in 1997 by the Libri group. Today, over 50,000 authors and 3,000 publishers use their services. BoD caters to German markets in Germany, Austria, Switzerland, but also to other Western European countries like France and Spain, as well as Scandinavian countries including Finland. Despite their international outlook, their website is only available in German.

BoD offer two publishing packages: eBooks only (free) or eBooks and print (€19). Both offer a free ISBN and the obligatory copy to the German National Library.

They require exclusivity, although you are allowed to sell your print books on your website and at events. BoD will be listed as your publisher, which does have the advantage that you can put their details in your Impressum without having to add your own address.

Be aware that if you publish with BoD, you're giving them your audio rights as well and won't be able to publish an audiobook while you're in contract with them. Your contract runs for one year, if you want to end this early, you'll have to pay a €149 fee.

BoD have various paid services on offer including editing, blurb writing, cover design, formatting, and various advertising/promotion options. One marketing tool that seems unique is being able to have your book shown at five different book stores of your choice (€69) or at the Frankfurt or Leipzig book fairs (€299).

***

**Distributes to:** over 1000 online retailers including all the main ones, tolino alliance. Option to distribute print books to international retailers.
**Can you exclude retailers?** no
**Royalty rate**: 70% of net royalties, 80% in their shop
**Fees**: free for eBooks, €19 for eBook + print
**Payment**: bank transfer
**Exclusivity**: yes
**ISBN**: yes, free
**Own store:** yes
**Print-on-demand**: yes
**Audiobooks**: no
**Website**: https://www.bod.de/
**Language:** German

## 12

## XINXII

**X**inxii is a Berlin-based distributor calling themselves "Europe's leading indie eBook self-publishing and distribution platform".

If you're direct with all the main retailers, the only other retailers you can choose at Xinxii are Casa del Libro, tolino (unless you're direct), e-Sentral and Scribd. Your book will also be available in their own store.

One thing you'll have to get used to is that XinXii doesn't pay automatically but by request. Once your confirmed revenue has reached €19.99, you can request payment via their dashboard.

The only marketing tool XinXii offers are free coupon codes that you can create in your dashboard (and an author page in their online shop).

**Distributes to:** all the main retailers incl the tolino alliance plus several others
**Can you exclude retailers?** yes
**Royalty rate**: up to 85% of net royalties, 40-70% of sales in their own store
**Fees**: none for fiction, €9.95 for non-fiction (€29.99 for audiobooks)
**Payment**: PayPal or bank transfer. By request once balance is over €19.99.
**Exclusivity**: no
**ISBN**: free
**Own store:** yes
**Print-on-demand**: no
**Audiobooks**: yes
**Website**: https://www.xinxii.de
**Language**: German, English

## RESOURCES

- Distribution overview: https://www.xinxii.com/global-ebook-sales-channels-57
- App for authors (Apple only): https://apps.apple.com/app/xinxii/id645485548

# FEIYR

F eiyr is a German distributor and the only one that offers both ebook, print-on-demand and audiobook distribution.

Their registration is probably the most difficult (or at least lengthy) of them all because they send you a letter via snail mail (yes, in an actual letter on actual paper) with an activation code. If you have a release coming up soon and plan to publish with Feiyr, apply for the account as soon as possible because it can take a few weeks to get that letter.

They charge an account activation cost of €9.90. Publishing ebooks is free, print books cost €9.90 each. If you request payment below €250, you pay a €2.50 transaction fee. Payments have to be requested in their dashboard, the minimum payment threshold is €25.

If you use their free ISBN, be aware that you'll have to mention them as publisher in the Impressum.

Feiyr offers a range of marketing tools. Free ones include an author page and download codes to give to readers. Paid options range from press releases (starting at €149) and NetGalley listings all the way to TV and film campaigns. They also have a free universal link tool called Link-it!, but you have to enter all retailer links individually so you might prefer an automatic tool like Books2Read (I certainly do).

My personal experience with Feiyr has been a bit of a nightmare. Here's an extract from a Facebook post I wrote about them in the Wide for the Win group:

> Your publication date has to be at least ten days in the future or they'll reject it. It doesn't seem to say that anywhere but I found out the hard way when they rejected my book and sent me a message.
>
> They give you tons of options when choosing categories based on several different systems. I guess that's a good thing to help readers find your books.
>
> They want their cover files BIG. I had to ask my designer to give me a version where the smallest side is at least 3000px.
>
> If you're like me and already reach a lot of other retailers direct, on the final page scroll down and accept the licence agreement **before** you untick some of the retailers. It doesn't work for me otherwise and I'll have to refresh the page.
>
> You can set up co-authors or contributors and have them paid via Feiyr directly. I'm planning

to try that with one book and see how it works.

Apparently you can have a free author page but it's refusing to let me upload an author picture and without that you can't create the homepage.

They don't know the difference between a subtitle and a tag line. I've spent all day trying to tell them that the tag line on my cover isn't my subtitle and that I therefore don't want to enter it in the subtitle field.

A bit more on that last point: they require your metadata to be exactly the same as what's on your cover. If you want to use a subtitle, it has to be on your cover. If you have a tagline and a subtitle on the cover, you're in trouble because you can't enter both in the metadata.

However, one advantage of Feiyr is their payment split feature which could be used to pay your translator if you have a royalty share agreement.

---

**Distributes to:** Around 200 retailers, full list here: https://www.feiyr.com/de/partner.html#category2
**Can you exclude retailers?** yes
**Royalty rate**: 80% of net royalties
**Fees**: €9.90 activation fee. Unpublishing a book costs €29.95.
**Payment**: bank transfer, Paypal (over €25)
**Exclusivity**: no
**ISBN**: free

**Own store:** no
**Print-on-demand**: yes, €9.90/book
**Audiobooks**: yes
**Website**: https://www.feiyr.com/
**Language**: German, English & others

---

## RESOURCES

- Universal link generator (registration needed): https://www.feiyr.com/de/link-it.html
- App: https://webapp.feiyr.com/

# EPUBLI

Looking at the epubli website is giving me a blast of nostalgia. I published my first ever book with them back in 2010. It was an anthology of stories created during a writing workshop for high school students. I had pretty much no idea what I was doing, although looking back, I'm impressed that my cover wasn't completely awful.

epubli belongs to the Holtzbrinck Publishing Group and is based in Berlin. Neobooks belongs to the same company, which is why you'll find these two distributors to be very similar.

epubli's exclusivity terms are a little more complicated than those of other distributors. You are allowed to publish your book elsewhere *if* it's a clearly recognisable other edition. This could be a large print book, a hardcover, a book with bonus content, etc. If you publish your eBook with epubli, you can publish the paperback elsewhere and vice versa.

For eBooks, you can opt to go direct with Amazon, but you can't exclude any other retailers.

**Distributes to:** all the main retailers, tolino alliance, subscription platforms like Skoobe and readfy
**Can you exclude retailers?** only Amazon
**Royalty rate**: 70% of net royalties
**Fees**: none
**Payment**: bank transfer
**Exclusivity**: not entirely (see above)
**ISBN**: free
**Own store:** no
**Print-on-demand**: yes
**Audiobooks**: no
**Website**: https://www.epubli.de
**Language:** German

## 15

# NEOBOOKS

Neobooks is a Berlin- based distributor belonging to the same publishing group as epubli.

At neobooks, you can only choose one retailer to be direct with (Amazon or Tolino), so if you want to be direct with several, neobooks isn't for you.

While they have a sleek dashboard for eBooks, for print books you have to send them your files and a questionnaire with your metadata by email. They're the only distributor offering print books who doesn't have a simple way of publishing them via a dashboard, which I find more than strange.

For print books, you can't use your own ISBN, you have to use the one neobooks provides for free. They will also be shown as the publisher (for eBooks and print books) on the book's product page.

neobooks offers authors the chance to be discovered by traditional publishers. During the publishing process, you can register your interest in this feature.

**Distributes to:** over 300 online retailers including Amazon, tolino alliance, subscription platforms
**Can you exclude retailers?** yes
**Royalty rate**: 70% of net royalties
**Fees**: none
**Payment**: bank transfer
**Exclusivity**: no
**ISBN**: free
**Own store:** no
**Print-on-demand**: yes (not on dashboard, has to be done manually)
**Audiobooks**: no
**Website**: https://www.neobooks.com/
**Language:** German

# BOOKRIX

B ookRix is a distributor based in Munich, Germany. They distribute to all the usual retailers including the tolino alliance, plus libraries and smaller stores.

BookRix only allows you to exclude Amazon, so if you want to be direct with other retailers, this distributor isn't an option for you.

---

**Distributes to:** all the main retailers, tolino alliance, plus smaller ones and libraries
**Can you exclude retailers?** Only Amazon
**Royalty rate**: 70% of net royalties
**Fees**: none
**Payment**: bank transfer (EU), PayPal (outside EU)
**Exclusivity**: no
**ISBN**: free
**Own store:** yes

**Print-on-demand**:
**Audiobooks**: no
**Website**: https://www.bookrix.de/
**Language**: German, English

# 17

# TREDITION

Tredition was published in 2006, making it one of the oldest self-publishing platforms in Germany. Over 20,000 authors have used them to distribute their books.

Tredition charges the highest fees of all the distributors. The publication of an ebook, paperback and hardcover costs €149,90 all together (which includes lots of marketing opportunities, see below). This fee is waived if you buy at least 35 author copies of your book. You don't have to do all three formats, but the price is the same even if you only want to publish your eBook with them.

You can make changes to your metadata or your book's content twice within the first 6 months of publication for free, after that it's €99.90.

Included in their package are free review copies for book shops, journalists, bloggers and influencers. Tredition also include free marketing including press releases, social media posts about new books, your own author and book website, and sending information about new releases to book retailers.

They also offer various paid author services like cover design, editing and formatting.

Tredition offer a royalty-share programme which you could use with your translator or co-authors.

---

**Distributes to:** all the main retailers incl tolino
**Can you exclude retailers?** yes
**Royalty rate**:
**Fees**: €149.90
**Payment**: bank transfer
**Exclusivity**: no
**Own store:** yes
https://tredition.de/buchshop/
**ISBN**: included
**Print-on-demand**: yes
**Audiobooks**: no
**Website**: https://tredition.com/
**Language: German, English**

# 18

# TWENTYSIX

TWENTYSIX is a German distributor whose name refers to the 26 letters of the alphabet. They love capital letters, as you'll see shortly.

While they were originally founded by Random House, TWENTYSIX was taken over by BoD in 2020 and had a complete reorganisation. They're now split into three imprints: LOVE, CRIME and EPIC (fantasy and science fiction).

EBook distribution is free, while the combination of eBook and print costs €39 (including two author copies). You can also splash out on their premium package for €199 which includes 10 author copies and a professional cover design.

All three packages include an ISBN as well as a book presentation in VLB-TIX, the title information system of German book retailers. TWENTYSIX say this will help advertising to book shops, bloggers, the media and readers.

If you distribute with TWENTYSIX, you have to be exclusive to them. If you choose the print package, you're giving away both your print **and** audiobook rights (just like with BoD), so only do this if you're not planning to produce audiobooks anytime soon. You are allowed to sell your books on your own website and at events.

As a new service (launching just before the release of this book, so I haven't been able to test it myself) they now offer free cover templates as part of their 'easyCOVER-Tool'.

Additionally, you can book both copy and line editing through their dashboard.

---

**Distributes to:** same as BoD
**Can you exclude retailers?** no
**Royalty rate**: 70% of net royalties
**Fees**: free for eBooks, €39 for eBook + print
**Payment**: bank transfer (min €25)
**Exclusivity**: yes
**ISBN**: yes, free
**Own store:** yes
**Print-on-demand**: yes
**Audiobooks**: no
**Website**: https://www.twentysix.de/
**Shop**: https://www.twentysix.de/shop/
**Language:** German

# BOOKMUNDO

**B**ookmundo is a co-operation between a network of German booksellers and the self-publishing company Mybestseller.

If you choose them as your distributor, you have two options:

1. Use their German Bookmundo site

2. Use their English Mybestseller site and inform them before pressing the publish button that you want your books to be sold in Germany.

> In your case it might be convenient to use mybestseller.co.uk and inform us that the book needs to be sold in Germany as well. The author can buy the own book which will be printed in the UK and can choose all German bookstores (Amazon cannot be excluded) and the Bookmundo webshop and a free author's

webshop. Books sold from those sales channels will be printed in Germany.

— BOOKMUNDO

Bookmundo offers authors to create their own online store. You'll get the same higher royalty rate for sales as you get in Bookmundo's own shop.

While they don't have a publishing fee as such, you do have to buy one of their ISBNs for €12.75 and can't use your own.

---

**Distributes to:** tolino, Amazon, Kobo, Ciando
**Can you exclude retailers?**
**Royalty rate**: depends on retailer, 44-50% of net sales price
**Fees**: none
**Payment**: bank transfer, PayPal
**Exclusivity**: no
**ISBN**: €12.75 (can't use your own)
**Own store:** yes (plus individual stores for authors)
https://publish.bookmundo.de/shop/
**Print-on-demand**: yes
**Audiobooks**: no
**Website**: https://www.bookmundo.de
**Language:** German (or use mybestseller.com in English)

# 20

# SMASHWORDS

Founded in 2007 by author Mark Coker, Smashwords is the world's largest distributor of indie books. Over half a million books have been published via the platform.

Smashwords don't distribute directly to any German retailers, but your books will reach the tolino alliance shops via Gardners, a UK book wholesaler.

While they have their own store, there is no way to filter by language, so I doubt many German speakers will buy books there.

---

**Distributes to:** all the main retailers (minus Google Play), libraries, smaller retailers worldwide, tolino (via Gardners)
**Can you exclude retailers?** yes
**Royalty rate**: 85% net royalties
**Fees**: none
**Payment**: PayPal, cheque (US only)
**Exclusivity**: no

**ISBN**: free
**Own store:** yes
**Print-on-demand**: no
**Audiobooks**: no
**Website**: https://www.smashwords.com/
**Language:** English

# 21

# PICK AND MIX

Unless you're planning to be exclusive with KDP, you have three options:

1. Go direct with all the large retailers and tolino themselves, then distributors for smaller retailers and libraries (Feiyr, XinXii or an English distributor).
2. Direct with only Amazon, then tolino, BookRix, epubli, neobooks or XinXii for everything else.
3. Go with one distributor for everything.

You could also publish via an English-language distributor like Draft2Digital, Publishdrive or Smashwords, but I'd recommend using a German one to get into all the smaller retailers international distributors might not work with. Of course, if you have time on your hands, you can always publish on all of them...

. . .

What I'm doing: Direct with Amazon, Kobo, Google Play, Apple and tolino. Draft2Digital for Barnes & Noble, libraries and some smaller retailers. Usually, I'm direct with B&N, but since they're US only, I decided to save some time since I'm not expecting many sales there. I've also uploaded my books to Feiyr, but results there have been disappointing, so I'm not sure yet if I will continue to do that - out of all retailers and distributors, this one takes the most effort.

## 3

# LIBRARIES AND SUBSCRIPTIONS

Not all readers will buy your eBook. Some will borrow it at a library or read it via a subscription platform. Flatrate platforms that promise unlimited books for a monthly fee are growing fast. Some, like Storytel, offer readers both eBooks and audiobooks, making the deal even more appealing.

## LIBRARIES

What's important to know is that just because you distribute your books to library platforms like Onleihe or Overdrive doesn't mean that readers can automatically borrow them. Libraries have to first buy your books before they're shown in their catalogue. Because of that, I've made it part of my routine to regularly encourage readers to ask for my books at their local library.

Some libraries work with a 'one copy, one user' (OCOU) model. They buy a copy of your book and only one reader can borrow it at a time. Just like with print books, they'd have to buy several copies of your book if they want to be able to have more than one reader borrow it at any one time.

A second model is 'cost per checkout' (CPC) where libraries don't have to buy a copy but instead pay you for each time a reader checks out your book.

I recommend setting your eBook price for libraries at about 2-3 times as much as you charge readers. tolino recommends to keep the price below €9.99.

There are two main library distribution options that you can access as a self-publisher: Onleihe and Overdrive.

## Onleihe

2.6 million people regularly borrow eBooks and other media like audiobooks from Germany's digital public library service Onleihe (powered by divibib). A study found that two thirds of them also *buy* books - which means they're your ideal target reader. They'll come across your book at the library and might then later buy the print version of it.

According to the same study, the majority of library borrowers are under 50 and tend to be female. They borrow an average of 14 eBooks and 9 audiobooks a year.

Tolino ereaders include Onleihe, meaning owners of the device can borrow books directly from their ereader.

You can reach Onleihe via tolino, BoD, Bookrix and Feiyr.

**OverDrive** has been providing eBooks to German libraries since 2014 and is partnered with Libreka, on of the largest distributors in Germany.

Libby is OverDrive's app that allows readers to borrow eBooks and audiobooks on the go.

You can get your books onto Overdrive via Kobo, Draft2Digital and several other distributors.

---

## SUBSCRIPTION PLATFORMS

Flatrate reading platforms are getting more and more popular all over the world, with readers used to getting unlimited entertainment via services such as Netflix.

There are several subscription services in the German market. The main ones are:

1. Kindle Unlimited - accessed via KDP, exclusivity required
2. tolino Select - via tolino
3. Skoobe - via tolino, Bookrix, epubli or Feiyr
4. Readfy - via BoD, epubli or Feiyr
5. Nextory - ebooks via Feiyr and Bookrix, audiobooks via Findaway Voices
6. Legimi - via Feiyr, epubli, neobooks, BoD and Bookrix
7. Storytel - audiobooks via Findaway Voices

Don't expect to earn much per sale/borrow from these platforms. Most of the time, you'll end up with less than

€0.50. It's all about quantity if you want to make money with subscription services.

You'll earn the most with Kindle Unlimited (depending on the length of your books), but they're also the only one requiring exclusivity.

*A note on Ready: it's free for readers and makes their money with ads - which means the payout for authors is horrendous. My books (distributed via Feiyr) made an average of €0.08 per sale. And yes, we're talking about full-length novels. After seeing that, I removed my books from Readfy.*

## RESOURCES

- Overview of subscription platforms on Selfpublisher Bibel (in German, from 2017): https://www.selfpublisherbibel.de/all-you-can-read-wie-selfpublisher-von-e-book-flatrates-profitieren/
- 2019 study about Onleihe (in English and German): https://www.boersenverein.de/markt-daten/marktforschung/studien-umfragen/studie-zur-onleihe-2019/
- tolino blog post about Onleihe (in German): https://blog.tolino-media.de/2019/11/mit-der-onleihe-in-die-virtuelle-bibliothek/

# 4

## FICTION APPS

I'm a big fan of fiction apps and a big chunk of my monthly book income comes from apps like Radish. Sadly, there aren't many similar options.

**Tapster Media GMBH** is a company with three fiction apps: Livory, Loverys (erotica) and Lively Story. All three of them offer chat stories, so you can't just upload the translation of your book. Livory and Loverys pay around €70 for a 1500-2000 word story.

https://tapster-media.com/

---

**Snipsl** is quite an unusual concept in that it offers readers sneak previews of books ('Schnipsel' means snippet) via an app. I tried it myself for my most recent translation, uploading the first few chapters in the months before release. I got a few likes, but I don't think it made any difference in terms of pre-orders.

The consensus among authors appears to be that Snipsl used to be effective especially for romance authors, but that it's now no longer worth the cost.

https://www.snipslmedia.de/

---

**Sweek** is a Wattpad-like platform where you can publish stories without getting paid for it. They also offer a print-on-demand service for your books.

https://sweek.com/

---

None of these three comes close to apps like Radish or KISS, but who knows, with more and more apps cropping up in the English-speaking market, maybe some of them will cater to German readers in the near future.

# PRINT BOOKS

# 22

## PRINT ON DEMAND

Just like with eBooks, there are several ways to get your print books into readers' hands. However, in this case, you don't want to choose between being Amazon-exclusive or wide. KDP Print doesn't require exclusivity, so you can mix and match distributors to your heart's content. At least in theory - ironically, several German print distributors want exclusivity.

The main print-on-demand services are:

- KDP Print (Amazon)
- BoD (we covered this in the distributor section)
- Epubli (again, already covered)
- Ingram Spark

Of these four, only KDP and Ingram Spark don't require exclusivity, so you could combine the two.

As further options, both Tredition and Feiyr offer print-on-demand for a fee. Draft2Digital has a print beta as well, but with limited trim sizes and no hardcovers.

Not all distributors offer the same trim sizes, so if you want a particular one, double check that before starting the publishing process. You can find more about trim sizes in the Formatting chapter.

---

## RESOURCES

- Indies Go German's overview of print (from 2016, slightly outdated): https://indiesgogerman.com/the-physical-book-market-in-germany-reach-german-bookstores-and-libraries/
- Comparison of print on demand providers on Indie-Autoren Bücher (in German): https://indie-autoren-buecher.de/selfpublishing-blog/selfpublishing-vergleich-der-kosten-und-margen-bei-printbuechern/

# KDP PRINT

K DP offers paperback and (currently in beta) hardcover print books. You don't need your own ISBN, but you can use your own if you want to.

When entering print book prices in KDP, you'll notice that the price you choose doesn't include VAT, so you have to adjust it slightly until the preview shows the price you want. For example, if you want a price of €9.99, you'll have to enter €9.34 as the list price.

Remember, you'll want pretty, professional looking prices, so make sure they end in .49 or .99.

KDP's expanded distribution isn't available for Germany, so even with that box ticked your print books won't be available in stores like Thalia.

*(Strangely enough, two of my KDP-only books show up on Thalia, but they seem to be exceptions.)*

Technically, book stores could order books at Amazon, but with this being their largest competitor who's threatening to take over the market, the chances of them doing so are very close to zero.

Going with just KDP Print is the easiest way to get a paperback version of your book, but I'd recommend combining it with a distributor like Ingram Spark.

# 24

# INGRAM SPARK

IngramSpark, a service operated by Lightning Source, has one of the largest global book distribution networks in the industry.

They send the information for your book to over 40,000 bookstores, libraries, and retailers in their global distribution network and lists the book as available for sale to them at a discounted price depending on the wholesale discount the publisher offers.

Because of the amount of places they distribute to, they are unable to provide a list of German retailers, but from experience I can say that my IngramSpark-distributed books show up on all the important ones like Thalia and Hugendubel.

While IngramSpark's main print locations are in the US, the UK and Australia, through their Global Connection programme, your books will be distributed to their German print partner Books on Demand (BoD). They will print and ship your books to retailers and customers. We'll take a closer look at BoD in the next chapter.

IngramSpark charges a $49 fee for both uploading and updating your book. You can get a free promo code to avoid this cost if you're a member of various author associations like the Alliance of Independent Authors (ALLI), Novelists, Inc. (NINC), Independent Book Publishers Association (IBPA) and others.

You will need your own ISBN, although US publishers can get a free one (however it can't be used in combination with a discount code, so it's either a free ISBN or free upload fees, but not both).

IngramSpark offers cover templates that you can send to your designer. Those templates include a barcode, so no need to generate that somewhere else.

*You can also publish ebooks through IngramSpark, however I recommend against that. The system is clunky, updates take forever and you can't pick and choose retailers, so it's an all-or-nothing platform.*

## RESOURCES

- Distribution: https://www.ingramspark.com/how-it-works/distribute
- Global Connection: https://help.ingramspark.com/hc/en-us/articles/210606203-Global-Connect-Program-GCP-#gcpm

- Distribution of Print Books: https://help. ingramspark.com/hc/en-us/articles/209072726- Distribution-of-Print-Books

## 25

# GETTING INTO BOOK STORES AND LIBRARIES

Once you've decided where to get your book printed, the next step is to bring it to readers. With Amazon being only a small part of the German print book market, you'll want to get your books into book shops and libraries.

While in your home country, you'd be able to go to your local book store and ask if they want to stock your book, it's a little harder when you're not in Germany and perhaps don't even speak the language.

Book stores and libraries get their information about what books are available from the VLB, the Verzeichnis Lieferbarer Bücher. The VLB has a publicly available database called buchhandel.de, which you can search for your book: https://www.buchhandel.de/

## THE VLB

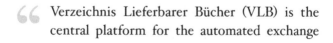 Verzeichnis Lieferbarer Bücher (VLB) is the central platform for the automated exchange

of product information in the German-language book industry. Based on global standards, on whose establishment and development the VLB has a significant influence, the system provides retailers and other customers with optimised metadata on approximately 2.5 million publications from more than 22,000 publishing firms.

— VLB.DE

You can register your titles with the VLB so that they can be found by book stores and librarians. It's not the easiest nor the quickest process, but if you want to sell more print books, this is the best way to do it.

If you use BoD , epubli or neobooks, they will do the registration for you since they act as your publisher.

**Important**: You can only register titles with ISBNs that you have bought yourself and that are registered to you. If you used KDP's free ISBN, you won't be able to add your book to the VLB.

Creating an account with the VLB is free and part of the website is in English. When I registered, they set up my legal name as a publisher and I had to get in touch with them to have that changed to my publisher name, so be aware of that.

They have a rather interesting fee model for registering your books. The more metadata you provide for each book, the cheaper it becomes. If you only enter the bare minimum, it costs you €5.10/book, but it can go down to €2.70/book if you give them more data. It becomes even cheaper if your book was published longer than three years ago.

However, there is an annual minimum fee of €69 (€99 if any of your titles don't have the 'gold' standard of metadata), so you'd have to enter a lot of books to pay more than that.

You can register eBooks, audiobooks and print books, although it makes the most sense for the latter.

Their dashboard is only available in German, which makes this a little more difficult for those authors who don't speak the language. Google Translate (other browser translation services are available) should help you manage, though.

Once you've registered a title, you're able to duplicate it, which comes in very handy for an alternative version of the same book or for multiple books in a series.

---

## RESOURCES

- VLB information (in English): https://vlb.de/en/services/titelmeldung and https://vlb.de/en/services/ihre-vorteile-1
- Sign up to the VLB (in German): https://vlb.de/leistungen/titelmeldung/registrierungsformular
- Help page for registering a title (you're going to need this!): https://vlb.de/hilfe/vlb-verlag/titelerfassung

- Buchhandel.de database: https://www.
  buchhandel.de/

You can find some excellent information about how to get your books into libraries (not specific to Germany) in 'Wide for the Win' by Mark Leslie Lefebvre.

# AUDIOBOOKS

# WHY AUDIOBOOKS?

40% of Germans listen to audiobooks at least occasionally (27% of Austrians) and the German audiobook market is worth 75 million Euro. Wouldn't you like a slice of that?

Audiobooks are especially worth considering if you write fiction or books for children and young adults: together, they make up over 80% of the market.

Producing an audiobook is generally more expensive in German than it is in English. Of course, a lot of it depends on the narrator's experience and popularity, but prepare to budget more for a German audiobook than you're used to.

While in English you usually calculate around 9000 words per finished hour (PFH), in German this reduces to around 8000 words.

To produce an audiobook, you can either find a narrator yourself, ask for auditions on ACX or Findaway Voices, or use a production company. In this part of the book, we'll take a closer look at all those options as well as distributors to bring your finished audiobook to your listeners.

There are five different ways you can earn money with audiobooks:

1. Sales at retailers (e.g. at Apple Books)
2. Subscriptions (e.g. at Audible, Scribd, Nextory)
3. Library sales and borrows
4. Streaming (e.g. Spotify) - makes up 30% of the market
5. Direct sales

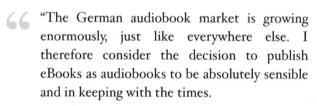

"The German audiobook market is growing enormously, just like everywhere else. I therefore consider the decision to publish eBooks as audiobooks to be absolutely sensible and in keeping with the times.

I have found that it is important to place audiobooks in as many shops as possible, not just Audible, because the trend is moving more and more towards the subscription/streaming model. Napster, Spotify, Bookbeat, Apple, Thalia music should definitely be included, as this covers most customer groups and age groups."

— MARLENE RAUCH, MISS MOTTE
PUBLISHER

At the time of writing, Kobo is the only retailer who lets you upload audiobooks directly. However, they don't sell audiobooks in their German store, so it's mostly irrelevant at the moment (I do recommend going direct with them for your English audiobooks, they've got great promotional opportunities).

If you have more than five audiobooks, you can try and contact Audible to go direct with them, but chances are they'll refer you to their ACX self-publishing platform.

For all other retailers, you have to go via a distributor.

# 27

# ACX

ACX is Amazon's own audiobook self-publishing platform that brings authors and narrators together. As an author, you can create a title profile and narrators will audition for the job. You can either pay upfront or go into a royalty-share arrangement with the narrator.

While ACX is great for English books, the main issue for German translations is finding good native speakers. Only narrators from some countries can register on the platform and Germany is currently excluded, meaning only German narrators living abroad in the US, UK, Canada or Ireland can be found there. In March 2019, ACX raised hoped by advertising for a senior project manager for Germany, but at the time of writing, ACX still isn't open to German narrators and authors.

When I set up an audiobook on ACX, at least two thirds were by non-native speakers (and truly awful). I also got several AI-narrated auditions. If you don't speak German, you'll need someone to listen to your auditions to give you feedback.

When producing through ACX, you have the option to be exclusive or non-exclusive to them. With the former, your book will be distributed to Amazon, Audible and Apple Books, and you'll get 40% royalties. You'll also be given review codes to hand to readers. If you decide against exclusivity, you can take your audiobook files and use them elsewhere, but you only get 25% royalties and no codes.

You can switch from one to the other after three months. Some authors like to do the first three months exclusively and then upload to other retailers afterwards.

**Pros**

- Can be one of the cheapest options depending on your narrator's rate
- You have full control over everything
- Going via ACX gives you the highest possible Audible royalty rate (if you're exclusive)

**Cons**

- Not many German narrators
- You'll have to deal with everything yourself
- Not easy to organise multi-narrator casts like dual or duet narration

Personally, I gave up after a while and decided to start my audio journey again when I had more time to search for narrators manually rather than go through ACX.

## RESOURCES

- ACX: https://www.acx.com/
- ACX University: https://acxuniversity.com/

## 28

# FINDAWAY VOICES

A s an audiobook production and distribution service, Findaway Voices is a great alternative to ACX. They distribute to over 40 retailers and libraries, including Audible, Apple Books, Google Play and many more.

You can use them for production and/or distribution. While ACX requires you to do most of the legwork yourself, Findaway Voices offers you more support, so if you're new to the world of audio, going with them will be the easier method.

When you set up your book on the platform, Findaway Voices will find narrators for you. You're able to specify what exactly you're looking for, like the age, accent, gender and general tone of your preferred narrator. They will then send you auditions from several narrators within 1-2 weeks.

PFH prices typically range from $150 to $300.

They also have a royalty split programme called Voices Share. In return for a 20% cut of your royalties, you can get the production for half the usual price.

Findaway pay 80% of net royalties.

If you've already got a narrator, you can use Findaway Voices for production without going through the audition process. And if you've got a finished audiobook, you can skip all that entirely and just use them for distribution.

German audiobooks are currently distributed to: Apple, Scribd, Nextory, Google Play, eStories, Follett, Authors Direct, and OverDrive. They also send German titles to Audible.com, but it is up to Audible.de to take the title. They don't send the titles directly to audible.de.

Sadly, Findaway Voices doesn't distribute to the Tolino alliance which means you're missing out on a substantial slice of the audio market.

They're constantly adding new partners though, so this might change in the future.

For a one-time fee, you can also set up your own audiobook store to sell direct to readers.

Here's mine as an example: https://shop.authors-direct.com/collections/skye-mackinnon

I usually combine ACX, Findaway Voices and Kobo for my audiobooks. I upload to ACX to get the highest possible non-exclusive Audible royalty rate (25%), upload directly to Kobo to have access to their promotions, and distribute to all the other retailers via Findaway Voices.

## RESOURCES

- Findaway Voices: https://findawayvoices.com
- Voices Share: https://support.findawayvoices.com/portal/en/kb/articles/what-is-voices-share
- Headphone report 2020 (pdf): https://my.findawayvoices.com/docs/FindawayVoices_2020_HeadphoneReport.pdf

# 29

# FINDING A NARRATOR

If you don't produce your audiobook via ACX or Findaway Voices, you will have to find your narrator in other ways.

There are various narrator databases or you can use a production company to deal with the entire process from start to finish.

## NARRATOR DATABASES

**Voices.com** has around 200 German-speaking narrators although not all of them are native speakers.

Voices.com

**Voice Rebels** is a German agency based in Munich with around 400 German speakers on their roster. You can either use their database to find a narrator and then sort out everything with them directly, or you can ask the agency to help you with the casting (and if needed with all other aspects of production).

https://www.voicerebels.de (in German)

**Voice123** is the world's first and largest narrator marketplace, having been founded in 2003. They have around 350 German-speaking voice actors, although not all of them are native speakers.

https://voice123.com

## PRODUCTION COMPANIES

*All three of these have reassured me that they can be contacted in English.*

**Voices for Books** has 10 regular German narrators plus another 10-20 they can call upon if needed. Their average PFH is $450 (including post-processing, mastering and quality control). The also offer translation into German for $0.15/word.

http://voicesforbooks.com/

**Deyan Audio** has over 60 German narrators, their PFH rates start at €680.

https://deyanaudio.com/

.  .  .

**Bee Audio** currently only has two German narrators but they're planning to add more soon. Their average PFH is $400-450 (including post-processing, mastering and quality control).

http://beeaudio.com

## 30

# AUDIO DISTRIBUTORS

Besides Findaway Voices, there are other distributors that offer to bring your audiobooks into retailers and library. Let's take a look at three of them.

## XINXII

We've already covered XinXii's ebook distribution, but they also offer to distribute your audiobooks to all the main retailers including the tolino alliance (Thalia, Weltbild, etc). You'll also get your own author store for free for readers to buy from you directly.

They charge a one-time processing fee of €29.99 which includes an ISBN.

Xinxii doesn't require exclusivity, so in theory, you can combine them with other distributors. However, you can't exclude any retailers when uploading a book.

Their website is available in German and English.

https://www.xinxii.de/publish-your-audiobook-with-xinxii-68

---

## FEIYR

Feiyr distributes audiobooks to Audible, Apple Books, the tolino alliance, Google Play, Spotify and several others.

You can find the full list here: https://www.feiyr.com/de/partner.html#category3

As mentioned in the earlier eBook section about Feiyr, they were set up catering to artists wanting to sell music tracks and it shows. Because they're used to albums consisting of songs, they don't see your audiobook as one product but as a combination of several tracks. In addition to a small publication fee (currently €2.36) you also have to pay a €0.49 ISRC fee for each track (International Standard Recording Code, basically an ISBN for audio recordings). If you haven't already got an account, it'll cost you a €9.90 activation fee.

You get 80% of net royalties.

Be aware that you can't change your audiobook files in the future.

Feiyr has recently introduced an audiobook production offer where they organise and pay for your production. Revenues are offset against the production cost and you'll only start earning royalties (50% of net revenue) once Feiyr has made their money back. If your audiobook makes less than the production cost, you won't have to pay them back.

You can apply for this opportunity through their dashboard.

---

## AUTHOR'S REPUBLIC

Author's Republic is a Canadian platform distributing to over 50 channels which include all the main retailers. They currently have three German-language partners: BookBeat, Skoobe and Divibib.

You can find the full list here: https://authorsrepublic. com/our-partners

There are no fees and you get 70% of net royalties.

If you choose to go with Author's Republic, you can't use another distributor for that book at the same time, although you can sell via ACX and your own website.

Let's look at three other companies that offer both distribution and audiobook production: Hörbuchmanufaktur, Miss Motte and Liberaudio. I've had a chat with all three of them and they're happy to be contacted in English.

---

## RESOURCES

Xinxii: https://www.xinxii.de/

Feiyr: http://www.feiyr.com/

Author's Republic: https://www.authorsrepublic.com/

# 31

# HÖRBUCHMANUFAKTUR

The Hörbuchmanufaktur (= audiobook factory) is an audiobook publisher based in Berlin, Germany. They've produced over 700 audiobooks for 238 authors and have around 30 narrators, including professional actors. They have studios across Germany.

They specialise in fiction, especially romance, thrillers, crime, urban fantasy and science fiction. The Hörbuchmanufaktur have their own event manager and often organise readings and live events for authors. They also help with retailer promotions and advertising, and provide videos of the narration process for you to use on social media.

They offer two royalty models:

1. 50% net royalties, you pay 50% of the cost
2. 20% net royalties, no cost to you

A finished audiobook hour costs €500 (plus VAT) and the contract is for five years.

Audiobooks will be sold at over 300 retailers, libraries and streaming platforms like Spotify and Deezer.

They gave me some examples of what they get as royalties from retailers to give you an idea of what you'll end up with.

- Audible: €2/borrow with subscription
- Retailers: around 60% of the sale price
- Streaming platforms: €0.003/track - here it's all about volume

You get paid every quarter.

The Hörbuchmanufaktur also offers a distribution-only model if you already have a finished audiobook, which includes an ISBN and sending a compulsory copy to the German National Library. They charge a €22 service fee and you'll receive 60% net royalties.

---

## RESOURCES

https://hoerbuchmanufaktur-berlin.de

Email: info@hoerbuchmanufaktur-berlin.de

## 32

# MISS MOTTE

**M**iss Motte (Miss Moth) is a German audiobook publisher founded by narrator Marlene Rauch. They work with around 70 narrators and handle all aspects of production and distribution, although you can also choose to just use them for the production. Miss Motte specialise in romance, erotica, young adult, fantasy, thrillers and science fiction. They're very happy to work with English-speaking authors.

As part of their process, you'll get sample narrations from selected narrators on their roster before you decide on a narrator (or narrators, they also offer dual narration). Their fee includes editing, mastering, proofing, etc and you'll be kept up to date throughout the process via an instant messaging platform.

Your finished audiobook will be distributed to all the major retailers as well as libraries and streaming platforms like Spotify and Napster. Miss Motte will also promote your audiobook on their social media channels.

The average PFH rate is around €430, plus/minus €100 depending on the narrator.

They also offer distribution of existing audiobooks for a 25% cut of net royalties.

Miss Motte pay once a quarter, although it's quite delayed compared to going direct with a distributor - for example, you won't get your royalties for the first quarter until early August.

---

## RESOURCES

Miss       Motte       website       (in       German): https://missmotteaudio.com

# 33

## LIBERAUDIO

Liberaudio is a publisher and distributor who distribute non-fiction audiobooks to over 50 retailers, libraries and streaming platforms including Audible.

They offer two royalty models:

1. 50% net royalties, you pay 50% of the production cost

2. 20% net royalties, no cost to you

3. You pay for the full production:

- Manuscript preparation (€70 PFH)
- Narrator fee (from €250 PFH)
- Sound engineering (€100 PFH)
- Quality control (€70 PFH)
- Service fee (from €250)

As an example, a 4 hour audiobook (around 32k words) would cost around €2,210.

You can also distribute your finished audiobook via Liberaudio. They require exclusivity, although you're allowed to sell your audiobook on your website.

Liberaudio have a marketing team that can support you with (paid) advertising campaigns which includes Facebook ads and advertising at various retailers. If you don't distribute via them, they can still help with Facebook ads.

---

## RESOURCES

Liberaudio website (in German): https://liberaudio.de

# MARKETING

# 1

## PROMOTE YOUR BOOK

Now that your book is ready and published, we turn to the issue of actually getting it into a reader's hands. As you'll know from your existing books, just because they *exist*, doesn't mean they sell. Remember, you've just become a new author again and need to build a platform from scratch.

In this part, we're looking at various methods to promote your books, both free and paid. This isn't reinventing the wheel - the basic elements like having a website, building a mailing list, running ads, are all the same as what you're used to. They just have to be tweaked a little to match the new language and audience.

Before we dive into the world of marketing, here's one of my favourite topics.

## UNIVERSAL LINKS

I'm a big fan of universal links. They transport readers right where they want to go: their own local storefront where they can one-click your book.

I personally use Books2read because it works for all ebook retailers as well as audiobook shops, plus it's free and easy to use, but there are many other options, both specifically designed ones for authors like Booklinker (Amazon only) or generic URL redirect services (make sure they have a geographic redirect option).

I've not found a German equivalent to Books2read, but they support all the important stores German readers will be looking for like Thalia, Hugendubel and Weltbild, so I've been using them anyway.

If your books are only on Amazon, you might be tempted to simply link to Amazon.de. But what about readers outside of Germany? Amazon doesn't automatically redirect to a user's marketplace.

When a reader outside Germany follows a .DE link, they can't just click the 'buy' button to get the book. On a computer, there's a manual redirect option and their local Amazon page is just one more click away. If they're on their phone, however, it's an entirely different matter. There is no handy button. The only way they can then get your book is to change the URL or to open the Amazon app to search for your book. Both of those use time. If I wasn't quite sure whether I'd like your book or not, I might not go through all that effort and forget about it.

By the way, it's only Amazon that gives you this much trouble. Kobo, iTunes and Google Play all redirect to your own country's storefront.

## 2

# PRICE PROMOTIONS

One of the easiest ways to attract new readers is by running a price promotion, either reducing your book's price to something like 99c or making it free. The latter could be for a longer period or even forever, making your book permafree, but I don't recommend keeping your book at 99c, even if it's the first in series. German readers are willing to pay higher prices for books than those in other markets and even frown upon such bargains (if it's cheap, the quality must be cheap).

Two thirds of the authors in my little research group said they'd run a limited time 99c sale.

Let's have a look at this and other services.

---

## BUCHDEALS

**Promotions:** free, reduced (at least by 50%) and new releases

**Reach:** 100k+ subscribers. On their website they state they have a 15-25% opening rate and a 5-8% click rate. Their emails only go to subscribers who've chosen that particular genre, with a max of 10 titles per email. They also list your deal on their website.

**Cost:** Buchdeals have various packages and offers. For their newsletter, reduced book deals are €59,90 and free deals are €37.90. A new release alert (can be at full price) costs. You can add an advert on their website (120k+ visitors a month) for €14.90/day. A push notification on their app will set you back €69.90 (70k+ active app users, 55k+ app push subscribers, 1k+ clicks per book). Their social media package is €19.90 and includes a Facebook post (7k likes) and an Instagram post (2k followers). They usually have around 2k impressions per post. Their most expensive add-on is a banner in their newsletter for €89.90 which will usually get 200 - 400 clicks per promotion.

If you don't want to book everything individually, they also have an all-inclusive package for €359. This includes two newsletter promotions, a banner on their website and a website push (where readers get a notification in their browser), a push notification in their app and social media posts, including ads.

All prices are plus 20% VAT.

If you're new to Buchdeals, you can use my affiliate code SKYEMACKINNON25 for €25 off your first booking.

**Payment methods:** Paypal, bank transfer

**Retailers:** Amazon, Thalia, Kobo, Google Play, Apple Books

**Language:** German and English

**Other info:** Buchdeals is special in that you can see your number of clicks after the promotion has finished. They also have length requirements for books and

After you book five promotions, you get free access to an online self-publishing course worth €399.

**Link**: https://buchdeals.de/autoren?locale=en

**Blog** (in German): https://autoren.buchdeals.de/

---

## KINDOFBOOK

**Promotions**: free and reduced

**Reach**: around 9k subscribers. According to their website, three quarters of their subscribers receive offers for all genres, the rest subscribed to specific genres only. They say you can assume your offer to reach around 85% of their subscribers, depending on genre.

**Cost**: Kindofbook uses BookPoints (BPs) as their currency. There's a chance they'll send your book to their list for free, but if you want to make sure, they charge 100 BPs. A second day costs 1,700 BPs and five days would set you back 6,800 BPs.

If you've already posted the same book in the past 12 months, prices will be higher.

100 BPs cost €1, although they also charge transaction costs and VAT (depending on your country). If you want to buy only 100 BPs, you'll end up paying €3.36. It's therefore recommended to buy points enough for several promotions at once to save on transaction costs.

**Payment methods**: Paypal and credit card

**Retailers**: Amazon only

**Language**: German and English

**Link**: https://uk.kindofbook.com/authors (English dashboard, be sure to click the German flag while booking a promo to choose Amazon DE)

**Other info**: You can also promote English books on Amazon UK and Amazon US with Kindofbook.

---

## WAS-LESE-ICH.DE

**Promotions**: free and reduced

**Reach**: unknown

**Cost**: free

**Retailers**: Amazon and option to enter ISBN for ebooks, paperbacks and hardcovers

**Language**: German

**Other info**: To set up a price promotion on was-lese-ich, you'll have to set up an account on their sister site rezi-suche.de which you can read more about in the Reviews chapter. That site is used for getting reviews from readers and bloggers (more about that later), but you use the same dashboard to notify them of a price promo.

---

## XTME

**Promotions**: free and reduced

**Reach**: 3k newsletter subscribers, 30k Facebook fans

**Cost**: It costs €9 to submit a free book deal. The website's owner then takes a look at it and if they think it's a good match, they'll post it on the website. If they don't, they'll send you an email explaining why, but you won't get your €9 back. If you want a sponsored ad, it's €19 for a standard one and €29 for a highlighted ad.

They also offer banner ads. The price depends on the size of the ad and starts at €9 for 1k impressions.

**Payment method:** Paypal

**Retailers**: Amazon, Thalia, Apple Books

**Language**: German

**Link**: https://www.xtme.de/ebookmeldung-fur-eine-gratisaktion

**Other info**: They also have a romance-only promo website, but it hasn't been updated since 2020: https://romance.xtme.de/

---

## BUCHFANS

**Promotions**: free and 99c

**Cost**: Free for book promo listings. You can also book a sponsored post or banner ad for €60 each (or €100 for both).

**Payment method:** Paypal

**Retailers**: Amazon

**Language**: German

**Link**: https://buchfans.com/leser-blogger-autoren/aktionen-gewinnspiele-melden

---

## BEST EBOOK FINDER

**Promotions**: free, reduced and full-price

**Reach**: 850 newsletter subscribers, 710 Instagram followers, 1000 Pinterest followers (no information on website visitors)

**Cost**: Their basic ad package costs €75 and includes a banner on their website for two weeks, the design of said banner, a Facebook post and inclusion in their newsletter.

They also offer banner ads on their website starting at €25.

**Retailers**: Amazon, tolino

**Language**: German

**Link**: https://bestebookfinder.de/werbung-auf-bestebookfinder/

---

## BUCHREGEN

**Promotions**: free and reduced

**Reach**: BuchRegen reaches around 600 website visitors/day, has 2.5k newsletter subscribers and 17.5k Facebook fans.

**Cost**: €37.50 for a promotion on Facebook, their website and in their newsletter.

**Payment method:** Paypal

**Retailers**: Amazon

**Language**: German

**Link**: https://buchregen.de/ebook-werbung-auf-buchregen

**Other info:** Books have to be longer than 150 pages. You'll have to apply seven or more days in advance. They also offer Facebook and Instagram ads.

---

## SCHNULZE DER WOCHE

(romance only)

**Promotions**: new releases

**Reach**: 10k likes on Facebook

**Cost**: free for 'Schnulze der Woche' (love story of the week) but they also offer paid advertising in the shape of giveaways, review requests, and more.

**Retailers**: Amazon

**Language**: German

**Link**: https://schnulze-der-woche.de/tipp-einreichen

# RETAILER PROMOTIONS

I f you run a price promotion, you can also get help from retailers to market your offer to readers. Some, like Apple, make it hard to get into their promos, while others, like tolino, couldn't be more happy to give your books a boost.

## AMAZON

Until recently, you were only able to get into Prime Reading and Kindle Deals if Amazon invited you. Now, you can apply for them directly via your KDP Dashboard. You need to be in KDP Select to apply for Prime Reading.

Occasionally, Amazon will also email authors directly with an invitation to join a promo.

## KOBO

Kobo Writing Life has a European team, but their focus isn't on Germany and they don't have a merchandiser for that market. They don't have promo opportunities for authors since they're partnered with tolino who're dominant in the German market.

## APPLE BOOKS

Apple have told me that they do offer promos for authors who're direct with them. However, to get into these, you need to already have their super-secret email address and I'm not allowed to share that. If you have an Apple rep or know that mysterious email address, you can get in touch and ask for promos just like you usually would for English books.

## TOLINO

tolino offers a range of in-house promos to indie authors who are direct with them. When I'd uploaded my first translation as a pre-order, I got in touch with them and asked if they could offer any promotion. They gave me not one, but six. In the end, my book was featured on Thalia, buecher.de, Weltbild and ebook.de. They also sent it in some sort of distributor newsletter and added it to their tolino Select e-book subscription service. All of this really helped with getting visibility on the tolino retailers and having a great launch as a 'new' author on the German market.

Of all the retailers I've worked with in the past, they were definitely the most helpful.

You can email them at publishing@tolino.media.

# 4

## SOCIAL MEDIA

Posting on social media is easy, right?

Not if you have to do it in a different language. Simply dropping a Facebook post into DeepL or Google Translate won't be enough.

Remember that steamy romance example? You don't want to describe your books in a way that doesn't make sense or is plain wrong. If your social media posts are full of mistakes, readers won't even bother clicking through to your book.

A way around this could be asking your translator to give you a bank of generic posts. Or hire a German PA. Or ask a reader or friend who speaks German.

When you start your German social media adventure, you can choose between two paths:

- Post German content on your existing accounts
- Create new accounts for German content

The latter will leave you with no audience, but once you find new followers, they will all be German readers. If you post in German on your existing channels, the chances of reaching your target audience are much lower.

Personally, I only created a German Facebook group and keep to my existing accounts for everything else. When I do a German post, I'll add a little German flag at the beginning to clearly mark it.

Less than a third of authors from my poll have a German social media presence.

Be aware of time zones when planning your social media posts. Germany, Austria and Switzerland use Central European Time (CET) which changes to Central European Summer Time (CEST) when daylight saving time comes into force. Be aware that the clocks change at different dates across the world.

On Facebook, you can use the inbuilt scheduling function, while for other platforms like Twitter and Instagram you can use a scheduling app like Hootsuite.

## FACEBOOK GROUPS

I'm not a fan of the drop-and-run method, but here is a selection of Facebook groups that let you freely advertise your books (all in German). Always check the rules in case this has changed.

https://www.facebook.com/groups/buechermelder

https://www.facebook.com/groups/buecherwerbung

https://www.facebook.com/groups/machdeinenlesedeal

https://www.facebook.com/groups/419602058769625

---

## HASHTAGS

Some generic book hashtags for Instagram and other social media include:

#buch #lesen #bücher #books #bücherwurm
#bücherliebe #buchempfehlung #buchblogger #read
#autor #leseratte #literatur #leseliebe
#lesenmachtglücklich

I recommend Tagsfinder to find more genre-specific hashtags.

https://www.tagsfinder.com/de-de/related/buch/

## 5

# BLOGS

Blogs still play a role in the German book world and there are a lot of active bloggers with either their own blogs or successful Facebook pages.

They're a great resource to network and to get book reviews, but it's one of the more time intensive ways of advertising your books.

The Self-publisher survey 2019 found that about a third of German indie authors work with bloggers.

You can find a regularly updated list of German book bloggers at Lesestunden.

Not all of them do reviews and some won't read books by indie authors. Many bloggers specialise in particular genres, so don't ask a thriller blogger to ask your steamy romance, you're waisting both your time.

Most bloggers prefer a print copy, which can be an issue when you live abroad. You could order a book at

Amazon.de, Thalia or a bookstore local to the blogger and have it sent straight to them.

---

## RESOURCES

- Lesestunden list of blogs: https://www.lesestunden.de/topliste/
- Rezi-suche blog list: https://rezi-suche.de/index/blogs.html

# 6

## WEBSITE

I wholeheartedly recommend setting up a website for your German books or at least a page on your existing website. This won't just give you somewhere to point your readers, but also with visibility and SEO (search engine optimisation).

When I only had one or two translations, I had a page readers could find in an 'other languages' drop down menu on my main page. Now, I have an entire website just for my German books. It's not as extensive as my English one (no blog or shop), but it's enough to give my German readers all the information they need:

- A page for each book (or at least for every series) with links to all retailers
- An 'about me' page with social media links
- Newsletter sign up
- Contact form

If you have just one page, clearly name the URL for the best SEO, e.g. authorname.com/deutsch or deutsch.authorname.com.

You should link to your website from within your books, on social media, in your newsletter, etc. My motto is to always prioritise linking to places where I can control everything - so while retailer links or universal links are fine occasionally, I prefer directing readers to my website.

Tip: If you're wide, you can add a tolino look-inside-the-book widget to your website. As an added bonus, you can add affiliate codes (AWIN and Tradedoubler).

https://affiliate.mytolino.com/index.html

# NEWSLETTER

I won't bore you by telling you what a newsletter is or why you should have one. I'm a big believer in the power of mailing lists and have put a lot of effort into growing and tending to mine.

Don't wait with setting up a mailing list until you're fully established in the German market. Even if you don't have much content to share at first, you'll want to gather those precious reader email addresses from the start.

Two thirds of the authors from my survey have a German newsletter and several others said they're planning to create one in the future.

Link to your newsletter everywhere you can: the beginning of your book, the end of your book, on your website, your retailer author pages (if possible), your social media accounts.

If you don't want to spend money on having a reader magnet translated (yet), you could use the first few chapters of your book. Or how about something else related to your book that's quick to translate like a recipe, a printable map, a certificate from the Intergalatic University (yes, that's one of mine).

Can you keep your existing newsletter provider? Technically, you can, as long as you make sure to translate everything into German, including your sign up forms, your opt-in confirmation email, your header and footer, and so on. Not all platforms will let you do that.

I use Mailchimp for my German mailing list because they have an integrated translation feature that automatically translates sign up forms. It also makes it easy to keep my mailing lists separate by using a different provider than I use for my English list.

Another option is Cleverreach which is available in both English and German. It seems to allow you to switch between languages and automatically translates sign up forms and standard texts for (I've not tried them myself yet).

When you send a newsletter, think of time zones! If you're in North America, your evening will be the middle of the night for Germany.

Tip: Send the sign-up link to your English mailing list (and post it on your social media channels). There might be some German speakers among your subscribers who'll sign up. It's how I got my first 100 or so subscribers - I already had them, I just didn't know it.

## GDPR

The European Union's privacy law, the General Data Protection Regulation (GDPR) came into force in May 2018. It aims to protect consumers and their data, which is great when you're the consumer, but it does present some restrictions for everyone wanting to sell something to the consumer. The law applies to all EU subscribers as well as UK subscribers since the UK now has their own version of GDPR.

> This Regulation lays down rules relating to the protection of natural persons with regard to the processing of personal data and rules relating to the free movement of personal data. This Regulation protects fundamental rights and freedoms of natural persons and in particular their right to the protection of personal data.
>
> — ARTICLE 1, GDPR

Ways to stay compliant with GDPR:

- Use double opt-in.
- Make it very clear what people are subscribing to and that they can unsubscribe at any time.
- Don't use pre-ticked consent boxes in your sign-up forms.
- Make it easy for people to unsubscribe .
- Don't use your subscribers' details for anything other than sending them emails.
- Keep records of your subscribers: where did they

subscribe, how did they consent, do you still have their consent.

- Data should be securely stored and not accessible to anyone else.

---

## RESOURCES

- Cleverreach: https://www.cleverreach.com/
- Mailchimp: https://mailchimp.com/
- Mailchimp help page about translating forms and content: https://mailchimp.com/help/manage-international-subscribers-in-mailchimp/
- GDPR - full legal text: https://gdpr-info.eu/

# 8

## GIFTING BOOKS

Sometimes, you might want to send a book to a reader, whether it's for the members of your street team, bloggers, giveaway winners or whatever else you can come up with.

Apple Books, Google Books, Kobo and some distributors give you the option to get free reviewer codes that you can pass on to readers. You'll have to email Kobo to get codes while the others have a tool built into their dashboards. This is particularly handy if you don't want to send eBook files directly.

If you want to gift a reader a book from Amazon.de, you have to be in the same country as them. If they're in Germany and you're not, you'll have to either send them direct to their Kindle or send the book via a service like Bookfunnel.

Alternatively, you could go to Amazon.de and buy a giftcard there.

(no, Amazon.com giftcards can't be used on Amazon.de)

---

## RESOURCES

Apple promo codes: https://itunespartner.apple.com/books/articles/apple-books-promo-codes-2740

Google Books promo codes: https://support.google.com/books/partner/answer/9827742?hl=en-GB&ref_topic=3238506

# REVIEWS

We all know how important reviews are in getting readers to buy our books. Besides asking at the end of your book or setting up a street team, there are several platforms that can help you connect with readers and send out review copies.

Ich würde mich sehr über eine Rezension freuen!
I'd love a review

## LOVELYBOOKS

The German equivalent to Goodreads is LovelyBooks. It offers authors the chance to conduct Leserunden (reading circles) where you provide a certain number of free books in the hope of getting reviews.

I've run several Leserunden on LovelyBooks and have been impressed by how many readers wrote reviews and interacted with me and other participants.

First, you'll have to create an author profile. To do so, make an account, then email info@lovelybooks.de with your username, your email address, your pen name and the ASIN or ISBN of your latest book. They'll then create an author profile for you within a couple of days. You can add videos and photos plus edit your bio and write a message to readers.

Once you have a profile, you can run your first reading circle. You decide how many books to give away and enter a bit of information about the book, then you'll wait for applications. I always ask applicants where they'll review the book so I can choose those who review on places other than just Amazon.

After selecting participants for your reading circle, you have to send them the book, either paperback or eBooks (specify which format you're offering in the initial description because some reviewers expect paperbacks). I use BookFunnel to send out eBooks.

You can run one Leserunde each month. If you want more than that, you'll have to pay a fee.


LovelyBooks in numbers (as of January 2021):

- Registered members: 350,000
- Authors and publishers: over 10,000
- Book reviews: over 80,000 each month
- Visits: 2.7 million each month, up to 100,000 each day
- Unique user: 1.9 million each month

You can also run ads on Lovelybooks, but those are expensive. The cheapest option, a newsletter and landing page ad costs €600, while the most expensive package will set you back €1,250.

## REZI-SUCHE

This platform aims to bring authors and bloggers together. Rezi is short for Rezension, review, and Suche means search. It's free for authors to add their books to the database and then either hope that bloggers will request a copy or be proactive and contact bloggers directly.

I've not had much luck with this site and looking at their list of submitted reviews, there hasn't been much activity in the past few months.

However, you might want to add your books to Rezi-Suche nonetheless because they also offer free promotion. If you're planning a sale or freebie, you can submit an entry which will then be published for free on was-lese-ich.

## REZILIEBE

Reziliebe is a Facebook group that connects authors with readers. You're able to offer review copies to readers who can then apply to receive one.

https://www.facebook.com/groups/573802799798363/

I've had a great experience with the group and will use them again for my upcoming releases. One reader even bought all my books in print afterwards, so I'd call that a success.

Don't post about your book yourself. Message one of the admins and provide them with the following:

- Cover
- Book title
- Your author name
- Is the book part of a series?
- Genre
- Page count
- Blurb
- Format and number of review copies
- When do you need the reviews? (they recommend a week per 100 pages)
- Where would you like reviews to be posted?

They will then post about your book and readers will apply in the comments. A few weeks later, they'll do another post where readers can link to their reviews.

---

## RESOURCES

- LovelyBooks: https://www.lovelybooks.de
- LovelyBooks help page about Leserunden (in German): https://www.lovelybooks.de/info/faq-fuer-autoren/?section=Leserunden%20Buchverlosungen
- LovelyBooks help page about author profiles (in German): https://www.lovelybooks.de/info/faq-fuer-autoren/?section=Autorenseiten
- Rezi-Suche: https://rezi-suche.de/
- Reziliebe Facebook group: https://www.facebook.com/groups/573802799798363/

# PAID ADS

E ntire books have been written about pay-per-click ads, so I won't reinvent the wheel here. The basic concepts are more or less the same for German books. You'll find that you'll have to spend less on ads directed at German readers.

Almost three quarters of the authors I talked to use Facebook ads and half use Amazon ads. They all paid less or the same than for ads for English books.

## AMAZON

When it was first possible to advertise on Amazon.de, bids were crazy low. I remember with fondness the days when you could get click costs below €0.05 and an ACOS of rarely above 10%.

Sadly, when Amazon opened this up to all KDP users, bids skyrocketed because authors used the recommended bid amounts, which were way higher than what was necessary.

This inflated costs and while it's still cheaper than running ads on Amazon US or UK, it's no longer as dirt cheap.

Moral of the story: do NOT use their suggested bids. Bid lower. If that doesn't work, you can always increase your bids, but whenever I run ads, I'm way beneath the suggested bids.

Amazon allows you to run sponsored product and sponsored brand ads on Amazon.de. You can access their platform via KDP (click on 'promote and advertise next to your book's entry on the dashboard, then choose Amazon.de from the 'Run an Ad Campaign' drop-down menu.

Alternatively, go to https://advertising.amazon.de.

## FACEBOOK

Again, you'll find Facebook ads targeting German-speaking readers cheaper than what you're used to.

Don't just advertise to German readers, include Austria and Switzerland as well. If you're wide, you might want to target owners of tolino devices.

If you want to know what German publishers and authors are doing, you can use the Facebook Ad Library to stalk them... I mean, to do research.

https://www.facebook.com/ads/library/

Set the location to Germany, choose 'all ads' from the drop down menu and then enter keywords like 'Autor', 'Verlag' (publisher) or a specific name into the search box. While it can be a good idea to do a generic search to see what ads looks like in German, you'll also want to look at authors who write in your genre.

---

But in the end, the next book is always the best advertising, so flick back to the first page and begin the process anew.

---

**Resources**

Guide to running ads on Amazon.de by Kindlepreneur: https://kindlepreneur.com/german-amazon-market/

# ACKNOWLEDGMENTS

*I hope this book has helped you in achieving your dream of getting your books translated and published in German. If you found it helpful, get in touch or write a review.*

I never thought I'd ever write a non-fiction book, least of all for fellow authors. Maybe, when I was still working as a science journalist, I would have considered working on some sort of sciencey book, but when I became a fiction author, any ambitions along those lines disappeared.

I'm telling you this because I was encouraged by some amazing people to share what I've learned. I didn't consider myself knowledgeable enough until they started asking me questions and pointed out that I knew a lot more about this topic than them.

Anyway, a big thank you goes to my fellow Wide for the Win admins (and friends) who've given me the confidence to be more than just a fiction author. Thank you Erin, Suzie, Adam and in extension Mark Leslie, Monica and Bradley.

Thank you everyone who's contributed to this book, especially Arno Lampmann, Renee Rott and Annette Kurz, who donated their time for an interview. I'm also sending a big Dankeschön to the authors who answered my survey and helped me gather data.

Apologies go to my three closest author friends who had to listen to my rants, self-doubts and general random thoughts: Arizona, Kelly and Laura. Without you, I wouldn't be where I am now (on all sorts of levels).

Thank you to my wonderful PA Tricia who held the fiction fort while I was dabbling in non-fiction.

And of course the biggest thanks goes to my cat, who graciously deleted a chapter that wasn't really needed. In her opinion, anyway.

*Skye B. MacKinnon*

# ABOUT THE AUTHOR

WRITING WITHOUT LIMITS

Skye B. MacKinnon is a non-fiction author who loves helping other writers succeed with self-publishing.

After a career in journalism and science communication, she now writes adult fiction full-time as USA Today bestselling author Skye MacKinnon. To relax, she also publishes children's books under her pen name Isla Wynter.

Having lived in various countries before settling in Scotland, she has a unique international perspective on publishing. Her books have been translated into five languages, including German.

perytonpress.com/skye_b_mackinnon

# PUBLISHING DICTIONARY

You can download a printable version of this dictionary from my website:
perytonpress.com/skye_b_mackinnon.html

Agentur - agency

Auflage - edition

Autor(in) - author (m/f)

Band - volume

Bellestrik - fiction book

Beschreibung - description, blurb

Buch/Bücher - book/books

Bucheinband - cover (also: Cover, Buchumschlag)

Buchpreisbindung - fixed price law

Buchrücken - (book) spine

Bücherei - library (also: Bibliothek)

Drucken - printing

Einleitung - introduction

Epilog - epilogue

Erscheinungstermin - release date

Fussnote - foot note

Gebundenes Buch - hardcover

Herausgeber - publisher

Herstellung - production

Hörbuch/Hörbücher - audiobook/audiobooks

Impressum - copyright information (in the front of a book), acknowledgements

Inhaltsverzeichnis - table of contents

Kapitel - chapter

Kategorie(n) - category/categories

Kinderbuch - children's book

Klappentext - blurb

Korrektor(in) - proofreader (m/f)

Korrektorat - proofreading

Kostenlos - free (also: gratis)

Lektor(in) - editor (m/f)

Lektorat - editing

Leser(in) - reader (m/f)

Liebesroman - romance novel

Nachwort - Afterword, Epilogue

Neuerscheinung - new release

Preis - price, prize

Preisaktion - price promotion

Preisbindung - fixed price

Prolog - prologue

Ratgeber - guide/self-help book

Rechnung - invoice

Reihe - series

Rezension - review (colloquial: Rezi)

Roman - novel

Sachbuch - non-fiction buch

Schreiben - writing; to write

Seite(n) - page(s)

Soziale Medien - social media

Taschenbuch - paperback

Testleser(in) - beta reader (m/f)

Titel (Buchtitel) - title (book title)

Titelschutz - title protection/copyright

Übersetzer(in) - translator (m/f)

Übersetzung - translation

Umsatzsteuer - VAT

Urheberrecht - copyright

Verkaufen - to sell; selling

Verlag - publisher (company)

Veröffentlichen - to publish

Veröffentlichung - Book release; publishing of a book

Vorwort - foreword

Vorschau - Preview

Werbung - advertising

Wettbewerb - competition

Widmung - dedication

## PHRASES

Now available - Jetzt erhältlich

New release - Neuerscheinung

Available at all retailers - überall im Handel erhältlich

Only €1 - Nur 1€ [note the currency sign is behind the number)

Anmerkung des Verfassers - Author's Note

## WORDS THAT ARE THE SAME

Barcode, Bestseller, Blog, Cover, Designer, eBook, Genre, Marketing, Newsletter, Self-Publishing, Website

Made in the USA
Las Vegas, NV
10 February 2022